RANKIN SCOTT KELLY

First Sheriff of El Paso County
— Colorado Territory —

RANKIN SCOTT KELLY
First Sheriff of El Paso County
— Colorado Territory —

John Wesley Anderson

Honoring the Past *Shaping the Future*

Circle Star Publishing
P. O. Box 60144
Colorado Springs, Colorado 80960

❦

ISBN: 978-1-943829-43-9

Library of Congress Control Number: 2022936335

Rankin Scott Kelly
Anderson, John Wesley
Revised Edition, April 15, 2022

Previously published by Old Colorado City Historical Society, 2017

Publisher's Cataloging-in-Publication data

Names: Anderson, John Wesley, 1954-, author.
Title: Rankin Scott Kelly : first sheriff of El Paso county , Colorado territory / John Wesley Anderson.
Description: Includes bibliographical references and index. | Colorado Springs, CO: Circle Star Publishing, an imprint of Rhyolite Press, LLC, 2022.
Identifiers: LCCN: 2022936335 | ISBN 978-1-943829-43-9
Subjects: LCSH Kelly, Rankin Scott. | Sheriffs--Colorado--El Paso Co.--Biography. | El Paso Co. (Colo.)--History. | Pioneers--Colorado--Biography. | Frontier and pioneer life--Colorado. | Colorado--History--To 1876. | BISAC BIOGRAPHY & AU-TOBIOGRAPHY / Historical | HISTORY / United States / 19th Century | HISTORY / United States / State & Local / West (AK, CA, CO, HI, ID, MT, NV, UT, WY)
Classification: LCC F784.C7 .A63 2022 | DDC 978.8/56/092--dc23

❦

Published and Printed in the United States of America

Cover photo: John W. Anderson 2021, Between Divide and Cripple Creek
Book layout/design: Susie Schorsch, cover design: Donald R.Kallaus
Circle Star Publishing is an imprint of Rhyolite Press LLC
Circle Star Publishing P.O. Box 60144 Colorado Springs, Colorado 80960

To the men and women of the
El Paso County Sheriff's Office
past, present and future

Titles By John Wesley Anderson

Non-Fiction

A to Z Colorado's Nearly Forgotten History, 1776-1876

Native American Prayer Trees of Colorado

Rankin Scott Kelly, First Sheriff, El Paso County, Colorado Territory

Ute Indian Prayer Trees of the Pikes Peak Region

Fiction

Sherlock Holmes in Little London, 1896 The Missing Year

ZacBox and the Pearls of Pleiades

R.S. Kelly, A Man of the Territory

Since the first publication of this book my desire to have El Paso County's first sheriff recognized has come to fruition. In 2017 the book received the Literary Award from the Historic Preservation Alliance of Colorado Springs and for that I am grateful. The Santa Fe Trail Association has also helped tremendously to preserve Rankin Scott Kelly's place in history. Thank you to the Old Colorado City Historical Society, the Pikes Peak Library District, and the Colorado Springs Pioneer Museum for their continued encouragement and support for this book and Colorado's history writers. A special thanks go to all those who supported the work on the Rocky Mountain PBS special, "The Sheriff" —it is comforting to know the life and service of El Paso County's first sheriff will not be forgotten.

Thank you,

John Wesley Anderson, Sheriff (ret.)
El Paso County, Colorado (1995-2003)

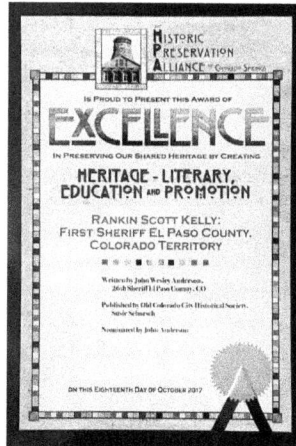

Table of Contents

An Honor Well Deserved

The Santa Fe Trail Association (SFTA) has long given recognition to those people who had an impact on or traveled the Santa Fe Trail prior to the 1900s. In January 2021, Rankin Scott Kelly, the first Sheriff of El Paso County, Colorado, received that honor, and was inducted into the Association's Historic Hall of Fame. The SFTA is a non-profit organization with the mission to protect and preserve the Santa Fe Trail and promote awareness of its historical legacy.

Rankin, who was known as Scott Kelly, was a teamster, carpenter and stonemason by trade. In the late spring of 1860, he traveled the Santa Fe Trail, along with a few other men, eight ox-drawn wagons, 48 head of cattle, and a large supply of provisions. They joined a wagon train of about 50 men, women and children, headed west on the Santa Fe Trail and arrived in (Old) Colorado City in the summer of 1860. The following year, when the Colorado Territory was established, Kelly was appointed the first Sheriff of El Paso County, where he served until 1867. Sheriff Kelly was involved in four shoot outs with outlaw gangs and had his horse shot out from under him—twice.

Rankin Scott Kelly was inducted into the SFTA Historic Hall of Fame in 2021 along with six other inductees, including Nestor Armijo, a highly successful second generation Hispano merchant who established businesses in Chihuahua and other Mexican cities; Charles Turnbull Hayden, who established a successful business delivering merchandise from Independence, Missouri, to Santa Fe, New Mexico; and John Van Deusen DuBois, an officer in the U.S. Army assigned to various forts in the Western Frontier, including Fort Union in 1858, where he led other soldiers in protecting travelers and the U.S. mail being transported along the Trail.

The Hall of Fame includes names that are known to history and some that would be lost if not for the efforts of individuals desiring to preserve history. Individuals who were previously inducted included William Becknell, who is credited with opening up the Santa Fe Trail for trade in 1821, Kit Carson, famous Indian Agent and U.S. Army Scout, and William Bent and Ceran St. Vrain, two of the founders of Bent's Old Fort.

Lesser-known individuals who have been recognized include: Mary Bernard Aguirre, known all her life as Mamie, (1844-1906) was born in St. Louis, Missouri. Her family moved back east to be by her mother's family. Prior to the Civil War they moved back to Missouri when Mamie was a young teenager. Her father was owner of a large store. She would return east to attend college before returning to Missouri. It was then she met and married Epifanio Aguirre, a prominent Mexican freighter. In 1863 Mamie embarked on her first of four to five trips down the Santa Fe Trail, traveling on to Las Cruces, New Mexico, and then to northern Mexico, where her husband's hacienda was located. Epifanio was killed in 1870 during an Indian ambush in south Arizona. Although Mamie took her three sons back to the Midwest, she returned to Arizona where she taught in rural schools until Apache threats forced her to abandon her post and move to Tucson. She was recruited by the University of Arizona to become their first woman professor.

Mamie was appointed head of the Spanish Language Department.

Also in the Hall of Fame are families such as the Hatch family, who traveled down the Santa Fe Trail to find a new life. Alexander and Lucy Hatch, with two of their three daughters and a son, traveled to Independence. Then, with a Webb and Doan wagon train, they went on to Santa Fe via the Cimarron Route, arriving in June 1848. Their third daughter and her husband followed the following spring with their two-year-old son and infant boy. They were involved in all of the major events during the American settlement of eastern New Mexico and Colorado. They operated the first hotel on the plaza in Las Vegas, New Mexico. They were homesteaders, ranchers, farmers and traders and established Hatch's Ranch in San Miguel County, New Mexico. They were engaged in the California and Colorado gold rushes, the Civil War, Plains Indian conflicts, and Comanchero trading.

The Hall of Fame contains people of all backgrounds, including Charlotte and Dick, a married slave couple belonging to William Bent. Recorded in many journals of those who visited Bent's Old Fort, are praises of Charlotte for her amazing cooking ability, her gift for entertaining guest and making people feel welcome at the fort. Charlotte loved to characterize herself as "de onlee lady in de dam Injun country." She brought cultured dancing to the dance floor, not the rude and wild dances of the frontier. She was in great demand as a partner by all. The last known of Charlotte and Dick was in 1847 when she and her husband left for Missouri as free persons. William Bent had granted both Charlotte and Dick their freedom in gratitude for Dick's bravery in the battle at Taos Pueblo which resulted in the defeat of the Indian rebels who had murdered William's brother Charles.

The Santa Fe Trail Association website contains a wealth of history of the over one hundred people who had a history with the trail and are included in the Hall of Fame. Not only do they honor those people who traveled the Trail prior to 1900, but also individuals who lived after 1900 who have made a significant contribution to the preservation of the Trail, historic information, artifacts or remnants related to the Trail.

Modern inductees were also honored in 2021, including Don and Doris Cress, who were organizers of many of the trail rides along the Trail, Richard Carrillo, an anthropologist and career archaeologist who worked to document and preserve the history of the Trail; and Mary A. and Leo E. Gamble, charter members of the SFTA who worked tirelessly to locate and maintain the historic markers along the Trail. These inductees, including Rankin Scott Kelly, were honored on Saturday September 26, 2021, during the SFTA 200-Year Anniversary Symposium closing banquet, held in the plaza of Bent's Old.

SANTA FE TRAIL ASSOCIATION

HALL OF FAME

ON THIS DATE, IN RECOGNITION OF HIS
HISTORY WITH THE TRAIL,
THE SANTA FE TRAIL ASSOCIATION
PROUDLY RECOGNIZES

Rankin Scott Kelly

WHO IS HEREBY INDUCTED INTO THE
SANTA FE TRAIL ASSOCIATION
HALL OF FAME

2021

I was honored to accept the Award on behalf of Rankin Scott Kelly, not only as the writer of this biography, but as retired member of law enforcement. Along with me at the SFTA Awards Ceremony were 88-year-old Dr. James Jefferson, Southern Ute Tribal Elder, the Great-grandson of Ute Chief Severo, and Don Kallaus, owner of Rhyolite Press, LLC, printer of the revised edition of this book *Rankin Scott Kelly, First Sheriff, El Paso County, Colorado Territory 1861-1867.*

— John Wesley Anderson, 26th Sheriff of El Paso County, Colorado.

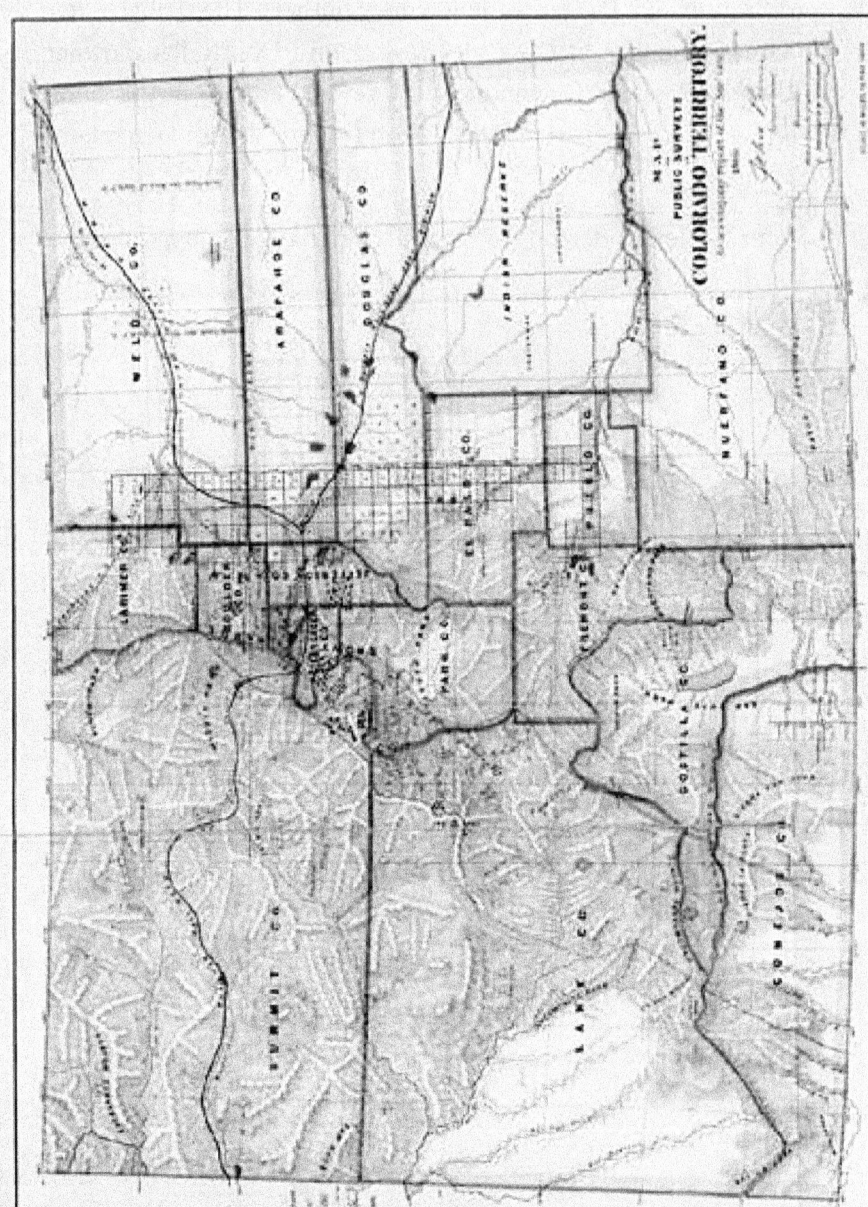

MAP
PUBLIC SURVEY
COLORADO TERRITORY.

1866 U.S. Government Land Office, CT Map

This early map of the Colorado Territory (CT) was commissioned by the United States Department of the Interior (DOI) Government Land Office. The map shows Colorado as known by Rankin Scott Kelly during his time as Sheriff. The map is of "Public Surveys in Colorado Territory" and released "to accompany the report of the Sur Gen 1866" under Commissioner J.S. Wilson and signed by John Pinner (sp) Surveyor General. It indicates the boundaries for the original 17 counties of the Colorado Territory, including El Paso County (which at the time included all of today's Teller County). This historic map captures a time before there were any major roads or highways. There is a fascinating trail represented by a dotted line that connects several counties and follows much of what is known of the old Indian trails. Pikes Peak (Pk) is depicted in the mountains of western El Paso County and the town of Colorado City (established in 1859) is shown with Fountaine que Bouille (today's Fountain Creek) running through the center of town. Two of the three routes that led to the 1859-1861 Pikes Peak Gold Rush, the Santa Fe Trail to the south and Smokey Hills Trail to the north, crossed over this Indian Reserve (the Oregon Trail was further north). Bent's Old Fort and Bent's (new) Fort are shown to the south of the Indian Reserve along the Arkansas River. The Ute Territory was generally accepted as being the western one-third of the Colorado Territory. In the upper left corner, the legend outlines the primary cause for the loss of land granted to the Ute people—the Developed Gold Region. This Developed Gold Region, which also listed the location of silver, copper, iron, and coal, along with the gulch (gold) diggings, was known as the Mineral Belt. Cutting across the upper portion of the Cheyenne and Arapaho Indian Reserve is the surveyed route for the Kansas Pacific Railroad General Palmer. (Map, Public domain)

Introduction

Law enforcement has always been in my blood. My mother was Colorado's first meter maid, hired in 1957 when the Colorado Springs Police Department (CSPD) first decided to use civilians other than police officers to issue parking tickets to cars parked illegally in the downtown area; a good source of revenue for the city, and a dependable source of income for a single mother raising three small children on her own. I was three years old at the time and vividly remember waving at my mother as she drove by the playground of my nursery school riding past wearing her tan uniform and sitting on her shiny white three-wheel Harley Davidson motorcycle. Another of my childhood heroes was my Uncle Harold "Red" Davis, a tough WWI Marine veteran who had earned a purple heart fighting in the south Pacific and captured my heart while stirring the imagination of myself and my other young cousins as we huddle beneath my Grandmother's dining room table at Thanksgiving and Christmas to listen to the war stories being told by the adults in the next room, several of whom were police officers. The respect I had for my mother, uncles, and cousins made me want to choose law enforcement as my profession prior to entering kindergarten.

My Uncle Red was a graduate of the prestigious North Western Traffic Institute in Evanston, Illinois, a town founded in 1857 and named after one of its founders, John Evans, who was appointed by President Abraham Lincoln to serve as the second Governor of the Colorado Territory. John Evans was very active in Republican politics in Abraham Lincoln's home state and Evans and Lincoln were personal friends. When then Sergeant Red Davis returned to Colorado Springs, he helped organize CSPD's first Traffic Division and hired their first meter maid, my mother, not knowing she would later be a member of his family. After learning my mother was raising three children on her own Red Davis introduced her to his younger brother Gary, who liked kids. Gary later married my mother. While they were on their short honeymoon, another of my law enforcement heroes, Uncle Red's younger brothers Les, took care of me and my sisters. My stepfather and mother went on to have two more girls of their own and adopted my only brother; a family of "yours mine and ours."

Uncle Red was promoted up the ranks to become one of only two Assistant Chiefs in the Department. When Police Chief Oren Boling announced his retirement and the other Assistant Chief, Carl Petry, announced he would be retiring soon himself, everyone was excited to see if Uncle Red would become the next CSPD Police Chief. I wasn't the only member of the Davis family or CSPD family to be disappointed when the City Manager passed over Uncle Red and selected a young Lieutenant to become the next Police Chief.

Uncle Red soon announced his retirement and I, a young CSPD police officer at the time, was truly heartbroken. Then to my utter astonishment just a few months later Uncle Red announced he was running for elected office to become the next El Paso County Sheriff. I hurriedly raced towards the Clerk and Recorders Office so I could register to vote for Uncle Red in the upcoming Primary Election; stopping briefly along the way to drop a dime in the pay phone to call my mother to ask which party I needed to register for to vote for Uncle Red. I'll never forget her sage words of advice, "well, you better vote

Republican or your Uncle Red may never speak to you again." Uncle Red won the general election, taking the seat away from a one-term Sheriff, becoming the 24th elected Sheriff for El Paso County, Colorado. Four years later Uncle Red was challenged by another Republican in the primary, one of my favorite college professors, Bernie Barry; however, easily won reelection. When my Uncle passed away, only partway through his second term, Bernie Barry was appointed and later reelected to serve as the 25th Sheriff of El Paso County. Heartbroken after Uncle Red's passing, I gave a fleeting thought that someday I might run for El Paso County Sheriff.

In the seventies, it seemed that people in law enforcement were always looking toward what was new and upcoming, but I was also interested in the history of the department. As police officers retired, I was occasionally handed a personal article as they cleaned out their desks or lockers and I tucked them away into boxes. While serving as a young police officer in the 1980s I was involved in writing an article remembering past police officers who had fallen in the line of duty. When the article came out I received a phone call at the Department from a local historian who chewed me out over the phone for not mentioning Chief of Detectives John Rowan who had been shot and killed on Friday the 13th of September, 1918, during a shootout in downtown Colorado Springs with the notorious Dale Jones Gang. Later, with the help of another young CSPD police officer, Joe Bonomo, we would add to the list of CSPD officers who died in the line of duty, Officer Benjamin Franklin Bish, who had been shot and killed in an alley in downtown Colorado Springs, attempting to apprehend two burglary suspects, on Sunday evening June 28th, 1896. This taught me again the importance of keeping historical records; it was hard to find all the officers killed in the line of duty due to alack of records.

One day Joe Bonomo came into my office and excitedly told me about a book project of the Colorado Springs Pioneer Museum. The book, *Here Lies Colorado Springs, Historical Figures Buried in Evergreen and Fairview Cemeteries* would highlight some of the people that were buried in either of the two city cemeteries. Joe and I decided we would submit the name of Officer Benjamin Franklin Bish and tell the story of how he was the first lawman in the Pikes Peak Region who gave his life in the line of duty. We were determined that his memory and his sacrifice would not be forgotten. We were elated when we were told that one of our own, a member of our law enforcement community, was not only selected for the book, but Officer Bish would be one of only ten people that would be highlighted when the book was launched. The people who had submitted the names and stories of the ten people chosen were given a book as a token of appreciation. Joe and I were honored to have been invited to attend the book launch in 1995 and beamed with pride as Officer Bish's service and sacrifice were retold. Another of the top ten honored in the book was Rankin Scott Kelly, the first sheriff of El Paso County whose story had been submitted by Ruth Willett Lanza. The one-page overview of his life recounting shootouts with outlaw gangs and the capture of a notorious Denver bank robber brought my imagination alive of what it would have been like to live in the 1860s, the time Kelly served as El Paso County's First Sheriff.

In November 1994 I was elected to serve as El Paso County's 26th County Sheriff. When I walked into the office for the first time on January 10, 1995, I sat down behind the same large wooden desk that my Uncle Red Davis had used during his time as Sheriff. I opened each of the large desk drawers, noticing that Sheriff Barry had carefully cleaned them out, and came across two small nondescript El Paso County Deputy Sheriff badges. I also found to my disappointment, the Sheriff's Office's attitude towards the preservation of the history of the Office was pretty much like I had experienced at the Police Department; everyone was so focused on new technologies, equipment, and development, that no one took much time to preserve their past. I decided that would change and collected three complete sets of badges, uniform patches, and award medals; one would hang in the Sheriff's Office, another I delivered to the Colorado Springs Pioneers Museum, and the third several members of my staff and I delivered to the Smithsonian Institute in Washington, D.C. I also made certain that our history was recorded in several ways, most especially in publishing our annual report for each of the eight years I served as El Paso County Sheriff. Copies of every annual report made their way into the Special Collections of various local museums and libraries.

While serving as Sheriff, a copy of the book *Here Lies Colorado Springs* was displayed proudly in my office, ever a reminder of our first sheriff whose memory would culminate with my desire to research and write a book on his life. Shortly after being elected to my first term, I shared with Ruth Lanza that I was interested in writing a book on Sheriff Kelly and was pleased when she sent to me in the mail her research notes on him. In studying the newspapers and other research notes she had collected over the years I saw she had relied heavily on the writings of Dora Foster, the daughter of Marcus A. Foster, a pioneer friend of Rankin Scott Kelly. I was certain I would be able to write the book on Sheriff Kelly in the eight years I served in office, but time flew by as my deputies and I were busy chasing down outlaws ourselves. As I look back with pride on the highlights of those eight years, the capstone of my thirty-year law enforcement career, I recall the day we arrested the man who kidnapped thirteen-year-old Heather Dawn Church, Robert Browne, who confessed to committing 49 murders in nine states across the western part of the country, and the day we captured five of the Texas 7, convicted murderers from Texas who had escaped from prison and murdered an Irving, Texas, police officer on Christmas Eve 2000.

The morning after I retired as El Paso County Sheriff, I reported for work at Lockheed Martin, one of the world's largest defense contractors. Certainly, without the duties of public office constantly demanding my time, I would be able to write Sheriff Kelly's story, right? Ten years working in Corporate America flew by just as fast as my time in public office.

On December 30th, 2013, my black lab, Mango, and I visited the gravesite of Rankin Scott Kelly in Evergreen Cemetery, to mark the 100th year anniversary of his passing. As Mango approached Sheriff

Kelly's gravesite she sniffed the ground above where he was laid to rest a century ago then laid down on the cool green grass next to his small gravestone as I placed the flowers we had brought. I still wanted to honor our pioneer sheriff and write a book. Another way to honor Kelly came to be before finishing the book. Rocky Mountain PBS asked for suggestions for topics for a series called Colorado Experience. I was delighted after submitting Sheriff Kelly as a topic that was accepted, but work on the book slowed as I worked with PBS.

As this book went to press, I wanted to make sure to invite Ruth Lanza to our upcoming book launch. She, along with Dora Foster, who had since long passed, was two of many people who through their early writings have helped us remember the life and honor the service of Kelly. I could not have adequately told his story without their research and reading their written words. Sadly, I discovered that shortly after Ruth Lanza had mailed me her original notes she passed away. I will be forever grateful to her and I hope you too enjoy reading about the story of the life of Rankin Scott Kelly and his dedicated service to the citizens of El Paso County, from 1861-1867, in the Colorado Territory of the American West.

Rankin Scott Kelly: This black and white photo was taken when Kelly was 87 years of age, a few months before his death in 1913. He is descending the west steps of what was at the time the El Paso County Administration Building. Today the building is the home of the Colorado Springs Pioneers Museum. (Courtesy, Special Collections, Colorado Springs Pioneers Museum. Photographer unknown.)

THE EARLY YEARS 1826–1860

Being a lawman in the early days of the American West took bravery, strength, ruthlessness, and a straight shot. Sometimes, the fine line between what was legally or morally right or wrong was crossed in the service of justice. In a time of lawlessness in the West, often the men who accepted the job of marshal or sheriff had lived on both sides of the fence, both outlaw and lawman. Early settlements in the West were wild rowdy places where honest men and women tried to scratch out a living among saloons, gambling halls, and brothels. Lawmen, generally, were honorable men and Rankin Scott Kelly was one of those men, although he too held a dark secret.

Aroostook County, Maine

He hadn't meant to kill him. There at his feet lay the bloody motionless body of Emitt, his older sister's finance. Just moments ago, fourteen-year-old Rankin Scott Kelly had been enjoying a midsummer's day walk with another boy, along the shoreline of a small lake near his family's home in Houlton, Maine. Kelly was anxious around water. His mother had drowned when he was two. Sister Katherine had stepped in to help raise her little brother, so their relationship was somewhat more complicated than most siblings. This might explain why Kelly's fear turned to anger as he watched Katherine, her friend, and Emitt out on the water in a small rowboat as it capsized. Rankin reacted in anger, though the tragedy of losing his mother would never legally justify his actions. Kelly knew all three were strong swimmers, but when he saw Emitt swimming to shore abandoning the two girls in the lake to fend for themselves, his anger blew up into an uncontrollable rage.

As Emitt waded ashore, Rankin met him with clenched fists, and then unleashed a fury of blows the older boy was not able to withstand. When Kelly finally backed away from Emitt's body, he heard no moaning sounds, saw no movement whatsoever; only the crimson blood flowing down his face. A bystander ran to Emitt and bent over his prostrate body to confirm Kelly's fears: Emitt was dead. Kelly looked down at his bloodstained hands, turned, and ran from the scene of his crime. For the next three days, Kelly wandered around the nearby foothills, sleeping in caves and contemplating his few options: turn himself in to face his punishment—almost certainly to be hanging— or run. He chose the latter. Kelly ran away from home intent on forever concealing his darkest secret. He knew he was wanted for murder. Kelly never returned to Maine, and never saw his family again. The events of young Kelly's life would not be known to others until shortly before Kelly's death in 1913 when he was interviewed by Dora Foster, a *Gazette Telegraph* reporter and author, who would publish her findings on Kelly in a collection of her memories, *Colorado Yesterdays* (copyright 1961).

Leaving home to find a new life was not new to the Kelly family. His father had emigrated from Ireland to Canada for the same reason. In Canada, he met the Canadian-English girl who would become his wife. Kelly's parents were married in New Brunswick, Canada, where his older brother, John, and sister, Katherine, was born. Rankin Scott Kelly was born on July 6, 1826, in Houlton; yet it remains unclear if he came to America or if America came to him. The 1910 U.S. Census would later record Rankin S. Kelly was naturalized a U.S. citizen in 1861, the same year Kelly became El Paso County's first sheriff. The town of Houlton had been settled by Joseph Houlton and Aaron Putnam in 1807 while it was still part of Massachusetts. Maine broke away from Massachusetts to become a state in 1820. Houlton was incorporated in 1831 and remains today the county seat for Aroostook County. By 1840, when Kelly ran away from home, Houlton was located just nine miles inside the fluid border of Maine, within the border of the United States.

Young Rankin was just 12 in 1838-1839 when the Aroostook War broke out between the United States and the United Kingdom; a dispute over where to draw the international boundary between the British colony of New Brunswick and the new state of Maine. Several American families had relocated into the Aroostook River Valley to harvest the virgin timber that grew along the west bank of the Saint

John River. Many British families had already settled along the east bank in New Brunswick, Canada, to harvest the virgin timber and cash in on the emerging lumber business, a business Kelly would pursue in his new home in Colorado. Lumbermen from New Brunswick and Maine were cutting more and more timber in the disputed territory, situated between England and its former colony, until tempers led to an armed confrontation on February 8, 1839.

The Mexican-American War and Heading West

Kelly's whereabouts from the time he ran away from home until he started west traveling the Santa Fe Trail in 1860 remains a mystery. Military records show Rankin S. Kelly enlisted on December 15, 1846, in Company B 1st Pennsylvania Infantry during the Mexican-American War. U.S. military forces were led by General Zachary Taylor to Texas, General Winfield Scott to Veracruz, Mexico, by sea, and by General Stephen Kearney down the Santa Fe Trail to secure the New Mexico Territory. The major campaigns during the first part of the war were the Texas Campaign (including battles fought at Palo Alto on May 8, 1846, and Resaca de la Palma on May 9, 1846), the California Campaign (1846-1847), the Northern Mexican Theater (including battles at Monterrey on September 21, 1846, and Buena Vista February 22-23, 1847), and the Mexico City Campaign (with battles at Vera Cruz, March 9-29, 1847, and Cerro Gordo on April 17, 1847).

Searches to determine which battles Kelly fought in have proved elusive; however, his date of discharge was listed on the Colorado Veterans' Graves Registration as April 4, 1847. It is likely that Kelly fought in more than one battle, and possibly in more than one campaign, although it does not appear, that he would have fought in any of the battles after Vera Cruz, March 9-29, 1847, because of the date of his discharge. After the city of Vera Cruz capitulated on March 27, 1847, following a devastating bombardment, hundreds of volunteers returned to the United States on a naval convoy under the command of Commodore Matthew C. Perry.

The Mexican-American War ended with the signing of the Treaty of Guadalupe Hidalgo on February 2, 1848. Mexico ceded the territory that is the present-day states of California, Nevada, Utah, New Mexico, and most of Arizona and Colorado. This war between Mexico and the United States would play later in Kelly's life when a Mexican family, living on land that had belonged to Mexico, believed they were ordained by Heaven to kill gringos and went on a killing spree in Colorado.

When Private Rankin S. Kelly initially enlisted to fight in the Mexican-American War, Stephen W. Kearney had just been promoted to brigadier general. On June 30, 1846, Kearney led a military force of around 2,500 men westward down the Santa Fe Trail into New Mexico. General Kearney used Bent's Old Fort (in what is now southeastern Colorado) as a military storehouse and hospital. Kelly served during the first part of the Mexican-American War (Dec 15, 1846–Apr 4, 1847); if he served under General Kearney this may have been Kelly's first introduction to the American West where Kelly would later return a dozen years later.

The Hollywood image of families riding west in covered wagons is largely a myth. The space inside a covered wagon was reserved for the most precious of cargoes. The only people allowed to ride in a covered wagon were babies or women who were about to deliver or had just delivered, a baby. A fortunate few may have ridden a mule or maybe a horse, but almost everyone who headed west walked. Kelly later explained to *Gazette* reporter Dora Foster that walking was easy for him, "I let my legs do the walking and do not try to make my whole body do it. In that way, I can walk all day without tiring myself."

Rankin Scott Kelly was one of nearly one-hundred-thousand people lured to the Pikes Peak Gold Rush in the mid-nineteenth century. He followed the Santa Fe Trail and then continued west to where the trail branched near Bent's Fort on the mountain branch. From Bent's Fort Kelly traveled west on the Cherokee Trail, which connected the Santa Fe Trail to the California-Oregon Trail. Travelers going "out west" had their choice of three established trail routes; each with its own unique set of perils. The Santa Fe Trail to the south followed the Arkansas River; the California-Oregon Trail to the north started along the Platte River and the lesser-traveled middle route of the two primary routes was the Smoky Hill Trail which followed the Smoky Hill fork west from the Kansas River.

Before arriving in the Pikes Peak region, Kelly made a living as a stonemason, carpenter, Indian fighter, and soldier. Later he became a miner. He also listed his profession as a teamster; sometimes called a bullwhacker. Bullwhackers walked beside the oxen that were pulling heavy freight wagons and used the crack of a whip and shouted commands to guide their teams.

Rankin Scott Kelly would later recount, "I came to Colorado June 5, 1860, with a wagon train of about 50 people of whom Robert Finley was one … William Booth was the wagon boss." Kelly was thirty-three when he arrived at the foot of Pikes Peak and was described as being tall and slender, with a shock of blond hair and piercing blue eyes. Inside the ox-drawn wagon that Kelly drove to the Pikes Peak area, when it was still part of the Kansas Territory, were the components for a 12-horse-powered steam-driven sawmill. The Finley Mill would be the first sawmill built in the Pikes Peak area. This sawmill was owned by Robert Finley and his business partners. Kelly delivered the first load of mill cut lumber to Colorado City.

Early explorers to what became the State of Colorado came to trap furs and trade with the Indians, and then the lure of gold and business opportunities brought settlement. The Pikes Peak Gold Rush had begun in July 1858 and peaked about the time the Colorado Territory was established on February 28, 1861, at the dawn of the American Civil War. The gold rush prospectors of the Colorado Territory, America's third major gold rush were called the "Fifty-Niners." Many of these early gold prospectors and miners had been "Forty-Niners" prospectors or miners who had taken part in the county's second major gold rush in California (1848-1855). The country's first major gold rush had been in 1829 on land under the control of the Cherokee Indians and was known as the Georgia Gold Rush.

Mining became the second major factor in the growing U.S. economy behind agriculture and mining drew hundreds of thousands of immigrants from all over the world, blending their combined ingenuity, labor, cultures, and individual talents to help unleash what would become the nation's third economic factor of economic growth: the Industrial Revolution. Technology was rapidly transforming this young nation and mobilizing its workforce in the nineteenth century. One minor problem that stood in the way of progress was the vast empty American desert west of the Mississippi River, which wasn't empty at all. It was the home to hundreds of thousands of the first Americans; Native Americans!

The American West in the mid-19th century was a vast uncharted region west of the muddy Mississippi River and extended to the crystal blue waters of the Pacific Ocean. Beyond the almost endless plains, filled with countless Indians hunting the American Bison, began the breathtakingly rugged Rocky Mountains, which extended to the west coast of the North American Continent. There, between the waters of the Mississippi and Pacific, lay the American West, a land of unfilled dreams. The rugged individuals, who traveled west to pursue their dreams, saw a vision of brown fertile farmland waiting to be plowed and green virgin forests waiting to be timbered, to build their ranches and raise their cattle. It was across this contested land that railroads and towns would spring up connecting America's east coast to its west.

By the time Rankin Scott Kelly headed west along the Santa Fe Trail in 1860, a distinct pattern had begun to emerge from the country's first two major gold rushes, whose prospectors had traversed the young nation from the Atlantic to the Pacific. The gold produced from

Georgia, beginning in 1828, peaked in 1829, then played out a few years later, much the same way that the gold in California discovered in 1848, peaked in 1849 and began to play out ten years later. By the mid-19th Century, the nation was experiencing an economic crisis. On November 24, 1857, the New York branch of the Ohio Life Insurance and Trust Company failed, launching the "Panic of 1857" that sent an economic shock wave rippling across the country. Stocks plummeted while unemployment soared, and the Panic of 1857 would lead to an economic depression that would last for three years.

Many men were desperate and out of work so not everyone who came west was looking to fulfill their dreams, many were simply trying to survive. When gold was discovered in 1858, 85 miles north of Pikes Peak, it didn't take long for gold fever to spread across the country. This third gold rush would peak a year later in 1859 and play out in a few years, at least temporarily. Another lesson that had been learned from the first two major gold rushes was that far more money could be made "mining the miners," that is, furnishing them the supplies they would require than would ever be extracted from the gold mines or found in the stream-beds. It was the discovery of gold that fueled westward expansion and lured men like Kelly west to make their fortunes culling the lumber from an area known as The Pineries that would be needed to build the Colorado Territory.

There were two initial groups of people responsible for establishing the Colorado Territory; the Greene Russell Party from Georgia who came to mine gold, followed by what became known as the Lawrence Party from eastern Kansas who were businessmen interested in the money that could be made through business ventures supporting the mining industry. Kelly was associated with the latter. His boss, Robert Finley, was one of the six original proprietors and incorporators of Olathe, Kansas in Johnson County directly across the Missouri River west of Independence, Missouri. Finley had been previously employed by the Johnson County Commissioners to serve as county surveyor. In 1859 Robert Finley bought an interest in a sawmill. When one of his business associates suggested their sawmill could do better if it were to be relocated further west to support the Pikes Peak Gold Rush, there wasn't much holding them back. Robert Finley resigned his office as county surveyor before his term had expired and began making preparations with his partners to dismantle and move the sawmill west. In early May of 1860, a party including Robert Finley, Scott Kelly, William Booth, George Smith, and Ambrose Furnoy started across the plains with forty-eight head of cattle, eight wagons, a large supply of provisions, and the twelve-horse power sawmill with all its machinery.

Moving west with the sawmill equipment was not easy. It would take nearly two months. Roads were not yet established causing many delays and finding water or a fresh horse was difficult. Westbound wagon trains often gathered at the trailhead to form up with larger caravans for safety in numbers out on the contested plains. One of the first duties of a wagon train preparing to strike out on the trail was to elect a wagon boss whose word was to be strictly followed. William Booth was elected the wagon boss for Finley and Kelly's wagon train and their trust in his leadership seemed to have been well placed.

Horse or mule teams may have been faster than oxen pulling a wagon, but oxen could pull heavier loads and they could eat grass while pulling a wagon so they would not have to stop to be unhitched to graze as they crossed the prairie grasslands. Every stop cost the party time and made them more susceptible to attack, especially the further out away from the trail and their main caravan that they were required to go to find sufficient grass for the livestock. Leaving too early in the season, in addition to being colder, was when the snow began to melt and cause the creeks to become swollen; teams often found themselves waiting for the waters to subside before they could attempt a crossing. One of the major disadvantages of leaving later in the summer was the grass closest to the trail was often overgrazed, sometimes all the way down to the ground, and teams that followed found themselves forced miles out away from the trail where they and their animals were more vulnerable to attack by Indians or wild animals.

To supply and protect travelers along the Santa Fe Trail before the gold rush of 1858 were a series of forts between Missouri and Santa Fe, including Fort Mann (1847), Fort Atkinson (1850), Fort Union (1851), Fort Larned (1859), and Fort Lyon (1860). The group that Kelly traveled with was not heading for Santa Fe and was following the Mountain Branch past Bent's Fort, a non-military fort, built for trading in 1833.

By the time Kelly reached the fork on the Santa Fe Trail at Bent's Fort, he had traveled 439 miles. As Kelly drove his yoke of oxen away from the ruins of Bent's Old Fort, they still had 80 miles to travel to reach the new town of Colorado City.

Twenty miles northeast of Colorado City in the Black Forest was the final destination for the Finley Sawmill, El Paso County's first, along Black Squirrel Creek adjacent to the Jimmy Camp Trail, also known at that location as the Cherokee Trail. Nothing remains today of the sawmill except a depression in the ground where once stood the main building of the Finley Sawmill established on June 16, 1861.

In October of 1859 Albert D. Richardson had written of his experience traveling to Colorado City where Kelly would arrive the following year:

> *Reached Colorado City, found a few weeks before, and containing fifteen or twenty log cabins… A morning visit to the curious Fontaine qui Bouille (fountains which boil) two miles from Colorado City, at the head of the creek I had followed up since leaving the Arkansas… The railroad will make the springs a popular summer resort. The vicinity combines more objects of interest and grandeur than any other spot on the continent: Pikes Peak, the great South Park, the Garden of the Gods, and the Fontaine qui Bouille.*

The Colorado City that greeted Kelly was but a few log cabins, no trains, few people, and very few roads. Colorado Springs would not be founded until 1871.

Robert Finley later sold his interest in the sawmill to business partners Jerome A. Weir and C.T. Judd, who had also come from the eastern Kansas Territory. The Weir Mill became very successful and supplied much of the lumber used to build Colorado City, the earliest homes and businesses in Colorado Springs, and the farms that soon sprung up in the Fountain Valley to the south. The Weir Mill stood about a mile east of where the east end of Shoup Road today comes to a dead end on Black Squirrel Creek, near the Cherokee Trail. Robert Finley had originally intended to return to Johnson County; however, he stayed on to become a well-respected Colorado City community leader and was elected El Paso County's first Treasurer. By the time the War Between the States had drawn to an end Robert Finley had sold his property in Kansas and become a prominent Colorado City businessman. In 1864 he traveled back down the Santa Fe Trail as a soldier with the 3rd regiment Colorado Volunteers to a place called Sand Creek. The Weir Mill in the Pineries, in the Black Forest, flourished and by the end of the century, it would be joined by two dozen more sawmills.

Of the remaining members of the party Kelly traveled with, the historical record reflects that William Booth moved on to Montana. Ambrose Furnoy moved to Canon City, where he was elected 10th Sheriff for Fremont County; however, he failed to qualify and resigned the office on December 30, 1868. It is unknown what happened to George Smith, but a George Smith was killed while riding next to Kelly during a shootout with outlaws when Kelly served as Sheriff.

Colorado City, Kansas Territory - Pikes Peak

Rankin Scott Kelly was 33 and in the prime of his life when he first walked down the dirt main street in Colorado City on June 5, 1860. The name of the street was and is today, Colorado Avenue. Colorado City, founded in 1859, would need lumber to grow, so opportunities for Finley's sawmill and a carpenter like Kelly were great. The founders of Colorado City were businessmen who saw opportunity and money to be made supplying the early miners that came to the area. Colorado City was established as a small gold mining supply town at the lower entrance to the Ute Pass, which had been traveled for centuries by the Ute Indians on their way to the summer hunting grounds in the mountains. The Colorado City Town Company retained Henry M. Fosdick, a well-educated engineer, to survey the plot and complete an engineering drawing of the townsite to be filed and used by the town's owners to market and develop their town. The map that Fosdick filed is today called the "Fosdick Plat." The below description of the town printed on the map for marketing purposes in 1860 shows the founders' hope for the area:

Colorado City is located at the base of Pike's Peak, at the mouth of the "Colorado Pass" the only wagon road for 70 miles north or south, to the South Park, Blue River, Tarry all, and Arkansas Gold mines. The famous Boiling Springs are only mile and a half distant. On the first of March 1860, there were 255 houses completed and many more contracted for. By reference to the U.S. Map, it will be observed that Colorado City is on the same parallel of latitude as Baltimore, Md., Cincinnati, O., Saint Louis and Kansas City, Mo., Lawrence and Fort Riley, Kansas, and San Francisco, Cal. Thus being one of the important cities that belt the continent & united the Atlantic with the Pacific.

A more accurate description of Colorado City can be found in the diary of Lucy Fosdick, the daughter of Henry Fosdick. She describes what her first home in early Colorado City looked like about the time Kelly arrived:

It had been built for a store and was a long, plain straight building with a door and two windows in the front, and with a door and one window in the back. It contained five rooms – kitchen, sitting room, and three bedrooms. The town consisted of one street, with a store and a few houses at the other end from where we lived. A desolate and forlorn place it must have appeared to my mother, coming from the luxuries of a New England life. The three cows that we had started from Lawrence had all come to untimely ends.

Truth be told, only about 80 people living in Colorado City at the time the Fosdick Plat was drawn up and no more than 200 buildings were built by the time Colorado Springs was established twelve years later. The tendency for town promoters to embellish was certainly nothing new; many of the Denver Town Company organizers were far more creative than those in Colorado City. The Colorado City townsite consisted of 1,280 acres containing 302 blocks divided into

9,874 lots with 18 streets 60 feet wide and two main east-west avenues 100 feet wide.

Without a sawmill, all the early buildings in Colorado City would have been built of logs; however, the interior floors, walls, or ceilings remained a construction challenge until mills like the Finley mill could produce the lumber needed. It was in this bustling environment that Scott Kelly, Robert Finley, William Booth, George Smith, and Ambrose Furnoy arrived with the components for the region's first sawmill. Lots in Colorado City were selling for $400 each. Men like Anthony Bott, M.S. Beach, Rufus Cable, George Bute, Henry Fosdick, Doc Garvin, and the Tappan Brothers were busy building cabins, barns, and businesses out of logs. Finley and his sawmill partners wasted no time in setting up their sawmill; becoming operational on June 16, 1860.

Kelly saw the promise in the Colorado City area too, which is evident from records of land purchases. Kelly bought several lots of land in the area. A year after being appointed the first sheriff for El Paso County, he had accumulated 17 lots in Colorado City; 5 of which he sold for $700 on March 23, 1862, to John Evans (believed to be the same John Evans who served as the second Colorado Territorial Governor, and who held a vast number of properties across Colorado). By 1861, a year after Kelly arrived in Colorado, he filed various claims for farming, ranching, and investment purposes in the area. One land claim was filed with the El Paso Claims Club to record the following:

> *Colorado City March 18th, 1861 Rankin S. Kelley claims within the jurisdiction of the El Paso Claim Club 160 acres of land for farming purposes described as follows to wit: Lying and being situated on the Fountaine Qui Bouille. Between five and six miles from Colorado City. As near as may be, and commending at a stake on the Southerly corner of James Garvin claim running thence southeasterly one half-mile to a stake: Thence northeasterly one-half mile across the creek to the Arkansas on Fountain City road. Thence one-half mile northwesterly along and near the*

said road: Thence one-half mile southwesterly across the creek
again to a stake, at the point of commencement. Said claim taken
and the foundation laid March 17th AD 1861. Rankin S. Kelley,
Witnessed by Fred Robert. Recorded March 18th, 1861 —A.S.
Cobb, Recorder T. Higgins Dept. March 18, 1863,

Another land claim filed on November 16, 1861, shows that Kelly
was also involved with working with a lime kiln. Not only did he
witness the recording of the land claim, but in a later interview with
Gazette reporter Dora Foster, Kelly said "I went to work at stonemason
work and burned the first kiln of lime that was burned on Bear Creek.
I worked at it in the summer of 1862. I built the stone building known
now as the Stockbridge Brewery. It was built for Emil Gehrung for a
dry goods and grocery."

An 800-acre estate that would become the future home of General
William Jackson Palmer, founder of Colorado Springs, was first owned
by Kelly. Palmer purchased it for $1,000 cash and began building his
castle named Glen Eyrie in a majestic canyon north of the Garden.

Kelly enjoyed life in Colorado City. The few settlers there came
together for holidays and social gatherings. The bachelor Scott Kelly
was described as a "natural" on the ballroom floor, and a very popular
dance partner with the ladies in Colorado City. As the evenings drew
to a close, all the other dancers would clear the ballroom floor and the
last dance, a varsovienne, was always reserved for Mrs. Lucy Maggard
and Scott Kelly. Lucy was one of the original pioneers in Colorado City.

Being single gave Kelly the freedom to do things he enjoyed while
not working at the mill, ranching, or building houses. He enjoyed
exploring the region and hunting. A Colorado College Professor, F.W.
Cragin, interviewed many of the early settlers to El Paso County and
later donated his interviews to the Colorado Springs Pioneers Museum.
One of the men he interviewed was Marcus A. Foster, the father of
Dora Foster, who would later write about Kelly's life. Professor Cragin
wrote this about Foster:

M.A. Foster came to Colorado City in 1860, arriving in Colorado City, El Paso County, in the spring of that year. In the fall of the same year, with Scott Kelly and Jack Ritchie, he went from Colorado City on a hunting and exploring trip over the mountains as far west as Mount Pisgah; crossing what afterward became the world-renowned gold district of Cripple Creek. They went by way of the Ute Pass route and returned by way of Ruxton Creek, passing the big Soda Spring, both going and coming; and it was between the date of his going and returning past the latter, that the log cabin was built at the Soda Springs, which was the first house built on the ground that later became the town-site of Manitou.

It was on this trip that Mr. Foster found Ouray – then a rising young chief of the Mountain Ute – sitting on the top of Mount Pisgah, watching through a field spy-glass the progress of a buffalo hunt in which some of his band were engaged. He conversed with Mr. Foster in a friendly way; but by and by sprang up and ran like a deer down the mountain, to intercept the game that seemed about to escape from the other hunters.

Although dancing, exploring and hunting were part of young Kelly's time in Colorado City, one of the most important things that filled his life was building. The lumber businesses that grew out of the Black Forest area is evidence of the quantity of lumber needed to support a growing El Paso County.

Based upon the chronology in Judy von Ahlefelt's book *Thunder, Sun and Snow, A History of Colorado's Black Forest*, nearly two dozen sawmills were built to harvest the trees from the virgin Black Forest: including:

El Paso County Sawmills

Date of Opening	Name	Location:
June 16, 1860	Robert Finley	Squirrel Creek
1863-66	Jerome A. Weir	Black Squirrel Creek

1864	Fleming Neff	Neff's Mill located on Neff's Gulch
1865-1870	Alden Bassett	3 Miles SE of Monument
1866-1878	Calvin Husted	Near Husted on Monument Creek
1866	Phillip P. Gomer	NE of Eastonville on Kiowa Creek
1875	H.C. Blakely	N of Monument
1870's	Wyman Blakewell	Location Unknown, in the Pinery
1878	Cornwell	S of Husted
1880-1900	Frank Agnew	5 Miles SE of Monument
1881	Woodland Lumber	2 Miles NE of Husted
1882-1902	Stewart McConnell	KK Ranch
1893	Hod Nichols	Kiowa Creek
Early 1900's	Huddle	Monument
1910-1920	Jim Durkee	SE Black Forest, W of Ayers Road
1920's	Trump	Trump Ranch (Park Forest Estates)
1920's	Edgar Lumber & Box	Shoup Road, W Black Forest
1920's	Norvell Mill	E of Hwy 83
1920's	Northrup Mill	W of Hwy 83, then Springs Valley
Unknown	Shoup Mill	Location Unknown
Unknown	G.W. Higby Mill	Location Unknown
Late 1920's	Dan Morris	Spruce Hill NW part of Black Forest
1930's	Achord	Table Rock Area

Early Steps towards Law Enforcement

Six weeks after arriving in Colorado City, Scott Kelly witnessed first-hand the violence associated with living in the West and the swiftness of frontier justice when Jim Laughlin shot Pat Devlin in Colorado City. A Colorado City historian, Colonel Dave Hughes, along with help from Madora Laughlin Boyd and Deanna Holcomb Bowman, researched what was one of the first shootouts in Colorado City and Kelly's first step in becoming part of El Paso County's law enforcement. Col. Hughes reported the findings in *West Word*, the newsletter of the Old Colorado City Historical Society.

James (Jim) Laughlin had been born in 1834 in Maryland. He and his wife Josephine traveled to the Rocky Mountains from the California goldfields after failing to strike it rich. Josephine was a well-educated lady and a schoolteacher originally from Clear Creek, Ohio. Jim had traveled to the gold camps west of Denver to sell supplies to the miners. He and Josephine had a baby boy named Denver. By 1860 the Laughlin's owned a 160-acre farm north of Colorado City beneath "Pope's Bluff" situated along the stagecoach road just north of present-day Garden of the Gods Road. Jim raised potatoes and hauled them to Denver by wagon to sell to support his family.

No one knew much about Pat Devlin before he arrived in town with a herd of cattle. How or where he had acquired the herd remains in doubt. Those who knew Devlin described him as a shady character; some say he had been a Kansas Raider, back in 1856, frequently crossing into Missouri for plunder, which might account for the herd of cattle. Devlin approached Laughlin with a business proposition; if he would allow Devlin to fatten up his cattle on Laughlin's ranch, come spring Devlin would drive the cattle over the Divide (present-day Monument Hill) to Denver and split the proceeds with Laughlin fifty-fifty. Laughlin agree and after the last snows had melted on the Divide, Devlin gathered up the herd and drove them north to Denver where they brought a nice profit.

Several days later Devlin returned to Laughlin's farm near Colorado City broke. He did have a lot of stories to tell about the wild times he had in Denver City. Laughlin, naturally upset at not being paid, confronted Devlin and an argument ensued. As tempers flared Devlin challenged Laughlin to a shootout. Jim Laughlin on the other hand was a peaceable man who didn't even own a gun. Devlin told him he'd better buy a gun and set a date for the shootout which he said would be in Colorado City.

On the day Devlin had chosen for the gunfight, Laughlin rode from his ranch following Camp Creek south down present-day 28th Street into Colorado City where he bought a gun, a 12-gauge double-barreled shotgun. Jim Laughlin waited in the alley behind the businesses on the north side of Colorado Avenue. Pat Devlin approached Colorado City and walked south down 28th Street toward Colorado Avenue. Devlin was heard by several citizens shouting that he had come to shoot Jim Laughlin; witnesses later suggested he was trying to draw a crowd so he could show off in front of them.

As Pat Devlin walked past the alley where Jim Laughlin waited, Laughlin stepped out from behind the business into the street and said to Devlin, "Good morning Pat." Devlin wheeled around and Laughlin fired both barrels. The self-professed quick-draw artist Pat Devlin never got off a shot. A crowd soon gathered and someone ran to fetch Doc Garvin, whose cabin was located a half-block away on the north side of Colorado Avenue. Devlin was carried to Doc Garvin's cabin while the El Paso Claims Club assembled in Colorado City. Judge Wagoner no doubt presided and the Claims Club members wasted no time in assembling a three-member jury drawn from the crowd who had assembled to try Jim Laughlin for the murder of Pat Devlin. The fact that Devlin was still alive was apparently viewed at the time as a mere technicality; everyone knew his wounds were so severe that he could not survive for long.

Scott Kelly was selected to serve as one of the jurors. Several witnesses testified that they had heard Pat Devlin threaten to shoot Jim Laughlin. It also appeared Laughlin had done what he could to comply with the Code of the West. He had first spoken to the other man before shooting him and he did not shoot him in the back. The jury took all of twenty minutes to acquit Laughlin of murder. Some remember the finding being self-defense; others say it was a justifiable homicide; whatever the case, Jim Laughlin soon returned home to his wife and their son.

Pat Devlin remained in Doc Garvin's cabin for the next two weeks, wretched in pain before succumbing to his shotgun wounds. As with many gunshot wounds inflicted in the West, victims more often than not died of lead poisoning than from the wounds themselves. Bullets were cast from lead and the black gunpowder was always dirty making it nearly impossible to completely clean the patient's wound tracks; twelve-gauge shotgun wounds were especially so. Scott Kelly claimed to have helped bury Pat Devlin, the first man killed in Colorado City. According to historian Dave Hughes, Devlin's body would have been carried up the hill behind Doc Garvin's cabin north of Colorado Avenue, likely just north of present-day 26th Street, where he was buried without fanfare.

Civil War on the Horizon

The New Year of 1861 started off with a cavalcade of violent events that would have unimaginable consequences for almost everyone living in North America at the time, including Rankin Scott Kelly. Of the thirty-four states comprising the United States, seven seceded from the union. Disputes in the western territories mounted. Sometimes simply mentioning the names Jefferson Davis or Abraham Lincoln invoked violence. Of the Pikes Peak gold-rushers living in the western Kansas Territory in 1861 at least 6,000 were Southern secessionists; one of every four in the Colorado Territory.

The U.S. Government's primary focus became the War Between the States, which allowed for growing violence in the West. In an attempt to curtail lawlessness out West, men were often recruited into law enforcement positions that were rarely trained and often may have walked on both sides of the law. Many men, including Rankin Scott Kelly, were running away from the law but were recruited because times were desperate and men who proved handy with a gun were in demand.

When President Lincoln appointed William Gilpin to serve as the first governor for the newly established Colorado Territory, he gave him one clear directive: make sure the Colorado Territory remains with the Union. Upon Gilpin's arrival in Denver, on May 27, 1861, he immediately went to work to make sure the Colorado Territory remained in the Union fold. Governor Gilpin would himself need to make a number of political appointments to help organize Colorado's Territorial government. To gain a better understanding of how to divide up the Territory into geographical districts, he first directed that a census be taken of the Colorado Territory. The census reported back that the Territory had a total population of 25,331, consisting of 20,758 white males, 4,484 white females, and 89 Negroes of both sexes. Gilpin then divided the Territory into semi-equal Districts and began appointing like-minded representatives from each District.

Although his tenure as the first Governor of the Colorado Territory would be short-lived, William Gilpin was a good choice for Colorado. American history may have been completely different had Gilpin not made the decisions that he made.

Governor Gilpin knew the Colorado Territory and knew the area as well or better than any other white man at the time. He was also unquestioningly loyal to President Lincoln; however, he knew that not everyone in the Colorado Territory in 1861 shared this loyalty to the President.

Three Confederate recruiting camps sprung up almost overnight in the Territory; at Mace's Hole in the Beulah Valley (western Pueblo County), another in the goldfields near Leadville (the gold camps in Alma and Fairplay). The third stronghold for Confederate recruiting was at Russellville, named after the Russel brothers (along Cherry Creek in southern Douglas County).

Further south in the Wet Mountains, 23 miles southwest of Pueblo, a large group of secessionists congregated and trained in 1861 in the Beulah Valley around Mace's Hole. This was an isolated forested area somewhat notorious as being a place where outlaws were known to have "holed up" until things "cooled down" after committing one of their many crimes. Beulah had been settled in the 1840s and is one of the oldest settlements in the West. It was originally named Fisher's

Hole, after Robert Fisher, a well-known fur trader, hunter, and guide. The name was changed to Mace's Hole in 1860 after Juan Mace, an outlaw and cattle rustler, hid out in the surrounding mountains. Word spread among secessionists across the Territory that men wanting to fight for the South needed to make their way to Mace's Hole. Within a few months, as many as 600 men had gathered near Beulah.

To defend the Colorado Territory from secessionists, Governor William Gilpin had been granted authorization to form the 1st Regimental Colorado Volunteers. On or about August 26, 1861, recruitment and commissions for the regiment officially began. Once the troops were organized, they were sent throughout the Colorado Territory to round up Confederates, beginning with the rebels at Mace's Hole.

Change was in the future for Colorado. The outbreak of the Civil War and the formation of the Colorado Territory would impact the early leaders elected to run the new counties, especially those men selected to serve in state and local law enforcement. Scott Kelly's life of avoiding his past and keeping a low profile to avoid the law was also about to take him in a new direction.

Sheriff's Job – Yesterday and Today

Comparing the job of Sheriff for El Paso County, Colorado, that Rankin Scott Kelly held in the mid-nineteenth century to what I encountered when I held the same office 142 years later makes me appreciate how some things never change and others have changed drastically. The basic needs to "move, shoot and communicate" remained essentially the same; however, how these needs were met couldn't be farther apart. Sheriff Kelly furnished his own horse, a fast gray mare, and gun. Today the Sheriff is issued a fast car and a gun.

When it came to communication, Sheriff Kelly was limited to essentially what someone told him in person, what he read in the Colorado City local weekly or Denver daily newspapers, or the occasional telegraph message sent by wire to Julesburg, Colorado, which is as far west as the telegraph lines ran until after the Civil War. From there the message was relayed to Denver City, then by stagecoach to Colorado City in a mail pouch. Communication was slow and unreliable, unlike today's radio, telephone, cell phone, wireless text messages, and email.

When Sheriff Kelly covered El Paso County, there were only a few small towns and there were no other lawmen, except for when the need arose. Then Sheriff Kelly had the power to deputize another man or could round up a posse. As the county grew, seven other towns and cities were established within El Paso County, eventually, most had their own police and fire departments, and when I was elected, the Colorado Springs Police Department employed more police officers than the Sheriff's Office. By 2003 when I retired, the Sheriff's office was staffed to cover a much larger population, but as in Kelly's time, the office still relied on volunteers like those who made up Kelly's posse. When I was Sheriff, nearly two hundred citizens volunteered to serve in specialized units including one of the premier Search and Rescue Units in Colorado, a highly trained Wildland Fire crew, the Sheriff's Chaplaincy Corp, a Victim's Advocacy Team, and a very dedicated part-time Sheriff's posse.

One large problem Kelly faced was the lack of a county jail. Prisoners were shackled in handcuffs and leg restraints until they could be brought before a judge or transported to Denver City where they were sometimes turned over to the U.S. Marshall for violations of federal crimes. In Denver and across the Territory it was easy for prisoners to escape and often because the facilities were full or nonexistent, prisoners that took great effort to track down were released or hung. As with most Sheriff's in the mid-19th century in the American West, Sheriff Kelly was responsible for all public safety duties and law enforcement responsibilities; these included everything from serving civil processes to fire suppression and even brand inspections. The Sheriff is still responsible for the civil process across the county (including serving court orders, such as restraining orders or mechanics liens); selling confiscated or seized property at periodic Sheriff's Sales. The Sheriff of El Paso rarely has to inspect cattle brands; however, it is still an important responsibility performed by many Sheriffs in the more rural areas of Colorado.

One interesting law still in existence from when the State of Colorado was first established is that by law the only person who can arrest a police chief from an incorporated city is the Sheriff. The only person who could arrest the Sheriff is the County Coroner. Another little-known law remaining on the books is establishing how much the Sheriff's wife can charge per day for feeding inmates housed in the county's jail. As Sheriff Kelly was unmarried this law didn't apply to him. My wife was less than enthusiastic about preparing three meals a day for 1200 prisoners, regardless of how much she might be reimbursed so it is a good thing that the law is not mandatory.

From Sheriff Kelly's time to mine, for some unexplainable reason, El Paso County still attracts the worst and most notorious criminals and outlaw gangs in the United States. Sheriff Kelly fought against the hostile Arapaho and the Cheyenne Dog Soldiers and had shootouts with outlaws like Salt Lake City Jim, Hank Way, Big Tooth Jim, and their gangs during the 1860s. Detectives, led by Captain Lou Smit, and I captured Robert Browne in 1995. Browne had kidnapped and murdered 13-year old Heather Dawn Church in northeastern El Paso County. Today he is serving two life sentences for first-degree murder. He also confessed to killing 49 people throughout the U.S. making him one of the most prolific serial killers in American history. In January 2001, the El Paso County SWAT team and I joined with the FBI and Teller County Sheriff's Office SWAT teams to help capture George Rivas and four of The Texas Seven, who had escaped from prison in Texas and murdered Irving Police Officer, Aubrey Hawkins, on Christmas Eve 2000.

When Sheriff Kelly needed assistance, as with the Hank Way Gang or hostile Indians who had gone on the warpath, if there was time, he could request assistance from one of the other 16 sheriffs in the Colorado Territory, or the Colorado 1st Regimental Volunteers, headquartered at Fort Weld, near Denver City. There was a U.S. Marshall stationed in Denver City, who when not transporting prisoners to Leavenworth, Kansas, might be called upon for assistance. Usually, there was not enough time to call on others or they were not readily available. Kelly often went out alone or with a posse of one other deputy. Much more reliable help is available today. Kelly would find that today's resources are seemingly unlimited, but he could always depend on his six-shot revolver, a fast horse, and Deputy Dan Gassenger.

Early view of Colorado City approximately 1868, shortly after Kelly served as sheriff. (Courtesy, Old Colorado City Historical Society, McKnight Collection)

SHERIFF RANKIN SCOTT KELLY
1861 – 1867

The first law enforcement agency to be organized in the Pikes Peak region was the Jefferson Mounted Rangers, modeled after the famed Texas Rangers who proudly wore the circle-star badge. These early lawmen, mostly volunteers, guarded gold shipments and helped keep the peace in the mining districts west of Denver City. Although this area was still part of the Kansas Territory the likelihood of any U.S. Marshall or soldiers arriving from Fort Leavenworth was virtually nonexistent. The 59'ers were pretty much on their own to organize themselves for self-defense or to maintain law and order; which is where the claims clubs came into play. When the Colorado Territory came into existence in 1861, the Jefferson Mounted Rangers became the Colorado Mounted Rangers and they remain in existence to this day donating thousands of volunteer hours annually to assist local law enforcement and other first responder agencies around the state.

El Paso County – Colorado Territory

The first Colorado General Legislative Assembly met in Denver on September 9, 1861, and over the next sixty days, their appointed Commissioners from each respective District met to enact laws for establishing the Colorado Territorial Government, including the passing of an Act to locate the capital of the Colorado Territory in Colorado City. Part of their rationale was that on a map Colorado City was located in the geographical center of the Territory; although some remember the men from the El Paso Claims Club encouraging their representative in Washington, Bill Williams, to push the southern boundary as far south as possible into the New Mexico Territory to create this effect. Based on geography and census population figures available at that time, legislation that named the county identified the county seat and defined the boundaries of the Colorado Territory divided into 17 original counties was agreed upon and signed by Governor Gilpin.

1.   Arapahoe, Denver: County named for predecessor Arapahoe County, Kansas Territory, which was named for the Arapaho Nation of Native Americans.

2. Boulder, Boulder: County named for the abundance of granite boulders along Boulder Creek.

3. Clear Creek, Idaho: County is named for Clear Creek, which originates in the county.

4. Conejos: Conejos is a historic site of a Hispano settlement. A major historical landmark of Conejos is the Our Lady of Guadalupe Parish Church, founded in 1858. Conejos is a Spanish word for "rabbit." Conejos County was believed to have also been referred to as Guadalupe County while the Colorado Territory was first being established.

5. Costilla, San Miguel: County named for the Costilla River. Costilla is a Spanish word meaning either little rib or furring timber.

6. Douglas, Frankstown: County named in honor of Stephen Arnold Douglas, U.S. Senator from Illinois from 1847 to 1861 (may have also been Douglas County, Kansas Territory).

7. El Paso, Colorado City: County named for Ute Pass in the country. El Paso is a Spanish term meaning "The Pass".

8. Fremont, Canon City: County named in honor of John Charles Fremont, the explorer, U.S. Army General, and later U.S. Senator from California.

9. Gilpin, Central City: County named in honor of William Gilpin, the first Governor of the Territory of Colorado.

10. Huerfano, Autubes: County named for Huerfano Butte, a solitary volcanic plug. Huerfano is a Spanish word meaning orphan.

11. Jefferson, Golden City: County named for its extralegal predecessor county, Jefferson County, Jefferson Territory, which in turn was named in honor of Thomas Jefferson, the author of the Declaration of independence and the third President of the United States.

12. Lake, Oro City: Named for the Twin Lakes in the county (Oro is another word for gold).

13. Larimer, Laporte: County named in honor of William Larimer, a pioneer entrepreneur.

14. Park, Tarryall City: County named for South Park, which occupies most of the county.

15. Pueblo, Pueblo: County named for the historic town of El Pueblo. Pueblo is a Spanish word meaning village or people.

16. Summit, Breckinridge: County named for the many high mountain summits in the area, and the county seat was established in November 1859 while still part of the Utah Territory. The town of Breckinridge was named after John C. Breckinridge of Kentucky, the 14th and the youngest Vice President of the United States; hoping the name would help them secure a U.S. Post Office, their plan paid off. After the Civil War broke out the former vice president sided with the south, becoming a brigadier general with the Confederate Army, and the town of Breckinridge changed the spelling of its name to "Breckenridge." John Breckinridge would later be affiliated with the pro-slavery secret society the Knights of the Golden Circle (KGC).

17. Weld, St. Vrain: Named in honor of Lewis Ledyard Weld, the first Secretary of the territory of Colorado.

When we think of El Paso County, we think in terms of what the county is today with Colorado Springs as its largest city. In Kelly's time as sheriff, Colorado Springs did not exist, nor did Manitou Springs. The town of Colorado City, now incorporated into the west side of Colorado Springs, was very small and surrounded by ranches and farms. The other main town was Fountain located in the Fountain Valley with Fountain Creek running through the townsite.

El Paso County, as it was originally laid out, was approximately forty by sixty miles (east-west), and encompassed the entire region around Pikes Peak. The altitude of El Paso County ranged in elevation from 5,095 feet above sea level on the southern border at Black Squirrel Creek to 14,115 feet on the summit of Pikes Peak. The headwaters of Black Squirrel Creek are further north in Black Forest with an elevation of 7,715 which makes this the highest point between the

Rocky Mountains and the Atlantic Ocean. When first established in 1861 El Paso County included all of the land currently located in El Paso and Teller Counties. Teller County was carved out of the western portion of El Paso County in 1899 and Cripple Creek was named as the county seat, during the height of the gold mining era at the end of the 19th Century. Present-day El Paso County consists of 2,159 square miles. This large county would be the area of jurisdiction for El Paso County's first sheriff.

On November 16, 1861, three El Paso County Commissioners appointed by Governor Gilpin met in Colorado City at the Tappan Mercantile Store located on the northwest corner of West Colorado Avenue and 28th Street. Tappan Mercantile was the first two-story frame building ever constructed in Colorado City. Alfred D. Sprague, Benjamin F. Crowell, and John Bley were elected to serve as the first County Commissioners for El Paso County. George A. Bute was appointed to serve as El Paso County's first County Clerk, Robert Finley was Treasurer, and Scott Kelly was appointed to serve as El Paso County Sheriff.

The three Commissioners agreed to secure a lease for $6 a month to rent the "Francisco House," a small one-story frame building that stood at what is today 2528 West Colorado Avenue. The building was not well insulated which caused the ink in the Clerk's ink well to freeze, so at the fourth meeting of the El Paso County Commissioners, on January 18, 1861, M.S. Beach recommended the county rent an office for the use of the clerk and other offices. The Commissioners approved his request and the El Paso County Clerk's records and furniture were moved into the small log cabin a block away, requiring all about thirty minutes to accomplish the task. This log building still exists; however, it was moved from its original location to Bancroft Park where it stands today in the 2500 block of West Colorado Avenue.

It can only be imagined what was in Kelly's mind as he accepted the appointment of Sheriff, knowing that he had fled his home in the East after he had committed the crime of murder and considered himself a fugitive. He would not be the first with such a past. Bat Masterson, Pat Garrett, Doc Holiday, and Wyatt Earp were all known Western lawmen. Bat Masterson's first gunfight caused by an argument about a woman, was when he was twenty-two. He killed both the man he was arguing with and the woman. Masterson decided to become a man of the law about this same time. Pat Garrett, elected sheriff of Lincoln County in 1880, initially was friends with Billy the Kid and they often gambled together. Garett later gained fame when he gunned down his former friend. Doc Holliday drank whiskey all day and was a skillful gambler, but is known as a famous Wild West lawman, always siding with his friend Wyatt Earp. It has been said that Holliday killed 16 to 30 men. Doc Holliday became skilled with guns and knives for self-protection. To be a successful gambler and to protect one's earnings it was helpful to enhance your reputation as a gunslinger. Doc's friend Wyatt Earp was a famous sheriff in Kansas before moving to Tombstone, Arizona, where he became a U.S. Marshall. Wyatt deputized many gunmen with dubious backgrounds and tough reputations to ride in a posse to protect his family and hunt the men who shot his brother. Rankin Scott Kelly was also a lawman with a past. He would be later known as a terror of desperadoes. Kelly successfully went after many outlaw gangs, often with just his deputy, and always came back successful.

Perhaps because of Kelly's desire to keep his past hidden he successfully avoided being counted in the 1840, 1850, and 1860 U.S. Census. He usually went by R. S. Kelly but his friends called him Scott Kelly. His last name was spelled, *Kelley* and *Kelly*. He was listed in the 1939 report by the Works Progress Association as a U.S. Veteran from 1846-47.

To understand what responsibilities Sheriff Kelly had just been appointed, it is important to understand who was living in El Paso County, what issues needed to be dealt with, and the geographical size of territory that he had to cover.

There was much the new sheriff would have to deal with. Land title disputes, theft, disputes between Northern and Southern sympathizers during the Civil War, fights and crimes committed due to the different nationalities living in the area that had changed hands from one nation to another; whether it be Spanish, Mexican, Native American, immigrants, or citizens of the United States. Cattle rustling, stagecoach robberies, and murders were a few of the more serious problems facing the new Sheriff. The enforcement of the law would be required before the West could be tamed, and Kelly would prove up to the challenge.

Gangs and Guns

One consistent crime in the American West was the theft of horses and livestock. Some herds were stolen by cattle rustlers and bandits, some by Native Americans, and some taken for the good of either the Northern cause or Southern cause. Sheriff Kelly took office at the beginning of the Civil War and many crimes in Colorado were caused due to the conflict over slavery and state's rights. Kelly would also serve during the height of the Indian Wars and theft by Native Americans would be so much a part of his life before, during, and after serving as Sheriff that often he referred to himself as an Indian fighter. To rustle cattle or rob stagecoaches usually required more than one person, so often thieves ran in small groups or gangs. Sheriff Kelly would deal with many of these as Sheriff. As he once told reporter Dora Foster:

> *Another time I followed some horse thieves down onto the Fountain to what is known as Bill Younger's ranch. From there I followed across into Mexico and on the other side of the Raton Mountains, known as the Red River in Mexico. I followed them for two miles before catching up with them at close quarters.*

They left the horses and hid in the brush. While I was getting the horses they shot my horse out from under me and I had some difficulty in getting out from under my horse and by that time it was getting dark. I lay in a small hollow all night without any bedding and no coat but I managed to get the saddle blanket off my dead horse and that was all the bedding I had that night. I suffered a good deal all that night from my leg that had been hurt when the horse fell on it. It pained me terribly but I managed to get the horses since they had gone off only a little way. I crept up to them and tied them together and led one. The men in the brush fired at me but I fired my shotgun into the brush where they were and that stopped them. They ceased firing.

The next morning I got onto one of the horses and struck the trail where they had started on foot but they went only a short distance when they took to the mountains. So I returned home. My leg was crippled for nearly a month.

Salt Lake City Jim Gang

Sheriff Kelly's first order of business was to deal with a gang of seven cattle rustlers and murderers known as the Salt Lake City Jim Gang who had set up camp near Colorado City on Monument Creek. The gang was well known for stealing open-range cattle that grazed in the lush grass along Monument Creek north of Fountain Creek. The cattle rustlers were reportedly butchering the cattle and then drying the beef which they sold as buffalo meat to the U.S. government at Camp Weld in Denver. Buffalo sold at a premium over beef cattle, so to some extent, the Salt Lake City Jim's Gang was also defrauding the federal government. Although much leaner than beef, the taste of buffalo can sometimes be difficult to discern; especially, it was said, if a quart of "Taos Lightning" or a bottle of "Oh Be Joyful" were to be found next to the sides of beef when the shipment was delivered, the quartermaster's taste buds were far less discerning.

Whether it was skill or simply the "luck of the Irish" or a little of each, we know that when Sheriff Kelly challenged the cattle rustlers and a deadly shootout ensued. Kelly was the victor. Of the seven members of the Salt Lake City Jim's Gang, El Paso County's new Sheriff killed two of the outlaws and wounded a third. History failed to capture which of the seven men were killed; however, the name "Salt Lake City Jim" was afterward dropped altogether from the historical record. Sheriff Kelly took his remaining five prisoners to Camp Weld where he turned them over to the U.S. government in Denver City. What happened to the prisoners from there is unknown; Leavenworth was six hundred miles away. More likely than not, these prisoners, like many others in the West, were offered an opportunity to swear an oath of allegiance to the Union and volunteer to fight in the northern army during the Civil War.

Hank Way Gang

While stationed temporarily in Colorado City, a sergeant from the 1st Colorado Cavalry and three privates were ordered to accompany Sheriff Kelly to help him arrest several horse thieves up on the Palmer Divide, at the headwaters of Kiowa Creek, where the outlaws were building a small fort near the eastern fringe of the Black Forest in northeastern El Paso County. Sheriff Kelly knew he was going to be out-gunned and requested assistance from the commanding cavalry officer after learning he would be going up against at least six outlaws and horse thieves known as the Hank Way Gang.

Sheriff Kelly explained what happened years later during the Foster interview:

In 1862 there were noted desperadoes who started stealing horses and they fixed a fort on the head of Kiowa Creek on the Divide. They built an underground stable that had a fort of logs in front of it for protection of themselves. They intented to steal horses wherever they could get them, store them for a while and then take them to Denver to sell them. Near there was a sawmill run by a man named Smith and one morning four of the thieves went to Mr. Smith's place and made him get them breakfast. After they had eaten they took all his provisions from him and then said, 'Now you rustle some more grub.'

Mr. Smith came to me and reported what had happened. At that time there happened to be about 20 soldiers stationed in the town and the commanding officer sent four of his men to go with me. We took horses and went after them one evening. The sergeant halted them and said, 'Come forth and surrender.' They had not yet finished the fort and at that time it was only about four feet high. They began to shoot at us, killing my horse at once, cutting off one stirrup, and striking the heel of my shoe. They shot the mill owner, Mr. Smith, killing him instantly. The sergeant returned the shot and put a bullet right thru the forehead of one of the robbers. He died then and there. Then the rest of them surrendered.

They were taken to Denver and the four soldiers put them in prison. Later, Col. Chivington had them take the oath of allegiance to the government and they were sent with some other soldiers to guard the paymaster in Fort Garland. Hank Way was the leader of the gang. Two days after reaching the fort, the four outlaws stole four government horses and set out for Butte, Montana. There they held up a passenger coach, relieving the passengers of all their money and express matter. They tried a second time; for this second time, they were all four killed. One man in the coach killed two of them but was killed in turn. The other passengers and the stage driver killed the other two and thus ended the Hank Way Gang. Bill Waggle was one of them killed at the John Riley fort but the other man I did not know.

When the Civil War first broke out, men in the Colorado Territory who wanted to volunteer to fight in the war departed immediately, thinking the war would not last long. Consequently, recruitment of men to serve in the Colorado Volunteers in the West, U.S. Territory, was difficult, which may be the reason for Chivington to "give the oath of allegiance" to Hank Way and the other three men in his gang. It is quite likely that they would have been pardoned first by Governor Evans before they were encouraged to enlist into the ranks of the Colorado Volunteers and then sent to Fort Garland to ironically guard the paymaster. It is doubtful Sheriff Kelly was surprised to learn the news of the robbery at Fort Garland by Hank Way or that his gang had held up two stagecoaches in Montana where they met their demise at the hands of a courageous passenger and the stagecoach drivers. Items found on the four men and their horses positively identified the four dead outlaws as the Hank Way gang and linked them to the robbery of the paymaster at Fort Garland.

One organized group of stagecoach and train robbers active in the West at the time were those men affiliated with the Knights of the Golden Circle (KGC). During the mid-19th Century, the KGC was organized as a pro-slavery secret society originally intended to annex a "golden circle" of territories that encircled Mexico (later to have been subdivided into 25 states), Central America, the northern portion of South America, Cuba and the rest of the Caribbean, for inclusion into the United States. All were to be admitted to the Union as slave states. Their ultimate goal was to increase the political power, wealth, and global influence of the Southern slave-holding upper class so they could never be toppled. In 1860 a convention of the KGC was held where they recognized the origins of their organization on July 4th, 1854 in Lexington, Kentucky.

Although details of how the Hank Way gang members were identified remain unknown, it is possible that what may have connected the four outlaws to the robbery of the paymaster at Fort Garland could have been the contents of saddlebags or the brands on the four stolen government horses. Horses that were ridden by U.S. Regular Army Cavalry troops were often branded on the left front shoulder with the capital letters US; except for the officers' horses, which were owned by the officers themselves. Military commissioned officers had to provide their own horses and revolvers, the enlisted troops were issued government horses and rifles, which they carried in a rifle scabbard attached to their saddles. The carbine rifles had a metal ring attached to a leather strap tied to the saddle in case the rifle was dropped it wouldn't be lost.

The cavalry horses that were branded with the capital letters US sometimes had a number associated with the brand. Branding irons were produced in sets with numbers 0 to 9, except there was no number 9; when the number 9 was needed the number 6 branding iron was used inverted. Some Calvary horses did carry the crossed sabers brand and sometimes it was shown as inverted crossed sabers.

As 1862 drew to an end, El Paso County Treasurer Robert Finley had collected a total of $138.00 and the Commissioners had voted to spend $105.10 leaving a balance in the El Paso County Treasury at year's end of $32.90. It is not clear how Sheriff Kelly was paid but early pioneer and writer Irving Howbert knew each of the men elected to work in El Paso County personally and later wrote in his autobiography, *Memories of a Lifetime in the Pikes Peak Region*. "All the county officers elected at that time were men of more than usual efficiency…without incurring any indebtedness whatsoever."

It remains unclear if the El Paso County Commissioners reimbursed Sheriff Kelly for his horse that was shot out from under him at the headwaters of Kiowa Creek by the Hank Way Gang. Sheriff Kelly later recounted that the County Commissioners occasionally paid for his expenses, and one source was discovered recording where he was reimbursed for buying rifles in Denver City which were distributed to citizens throughout the county during the 1864 and 1868 Indian Wars. The horse Sheriff Kelly was riding during the gunfight with the Hank Way Gang was the first horse to be shot out from under the El Paso County Sheriff by outlaws, but it would not be his last.

Espinosa Gang

The inscription on a Territory gravestone, protected by a weathered white picket fence, reads, "Henry Harkens, Murdered Wednesday Eve., March 18, 1863." The grave rests on a small grass-covered mound below a magnificent red rock canyon wall millions of years old. It is known as "Dead Man's Canyon." The gravesite marks the beginning of one of the darkest crime sprees in the history of the Colorado Territory. Similar to Scott Kelly, Henry Harkens had helped relocate the components for a sawmill traveling on the Santa Fe Trail by wagon train. Henry and his friends were also building a small log cabin where they were to live while operating the sawmill in southern El Paso County. Henry was the third known murder victim of the notorious Espinosa brothers. He was not their last; the Espinosas were just getting started.

The Espinosa brother's crime spree is worthy of note, although very little is known regarding any action Sheriff Kelly played in the hunt for the criminals. It is known that he was notified of the murders of Henry Harkens and Franklin Bruce, and immediately selected one deputy to join in the manhunt for the Espinosa brothers. A Mrs. Priest was interviewed years later by the *Colorado Springs Gazette Telegraph* and recalled how on the day after Henry's murder, March 19, 1863, while the neighbors dug a grave for Harkens, she saw two horsemen approaching. A newspaper article, published on December 30, 1930, quoted Mrs. Priest as saying, "It was Sheriff (Scott) Kelly (of El Paso County) and his deputy. He told us an unknown gang had (also) killed a man on Hardscrabble Creek. They didn't wait long and were headed off on the trail of the bandits." Kelly's job would often require him to gather a posse and hunt criminals, as in the case of the Espinosa brothers who were hunted throughout the Colorado Territory.

The Espinosa Gang admitted to killing thirty-two people, but the number may have been higher. Their killing spree began when the brothers were identified as having robbed a freight wagon delivering supplies from Santa Fe to a priest in Southern Colorado. A small cavalry unit from Ft. Garland was detailed to accompany Deputy U.S.

Marshall George Austen to the Espinosa ranch in the San Louis Valley. A gunfight erupted and a corporal was killed. Felipe and his brother Vivian escaped. Felipe claimed he had seen a vision of the Virgin Mary who told him to kill as many "gringos" as possible. His anti-Anglo vendetta got its roots in the Mexican American War. It was only twelve years earlier that Mexico had lost the territory where the Espinosa family had their farm. Although they were now American citizens, they, like many Mexicans, were treated by many as second-class citizens.

The brothers escaped north up through El Paso County and on toward Fairplay, murdering and robbing along the way. Vivian was killed, and Felipe recruited his nephew Juan Espinosa to join the gang to avenge Vivian's death.

Although many were on the hunt for the Espinosa Gang, Colonel Sam Tappan, the garrison commander at Fort Garland, hired Tom Tobin, a well-known tracker, to help hunt down the gang. Tobin was successful and shot both Felipe and Juan dead. Tobin beheaded them and delivered their heads to the garrison commander to collect the reward.

Kelly's Guns

A sheriff's most important equipment included a fast horse, a place to hold prisoners, and last but not least, his guns.

We know Kelly had a fast horse due to a report given by one Colorado City resident talking about a favorite pastime during the 1860s, horse racing. One resident, Mr. Buzzard, recalled several races including one race between a horse owned by Seph Sheidler and another owned by Frank Flannegan; Buzzard won $500 from J.B. Riggs on that race. Many of the horse races were held on the mesa above Colorado City where the men built a one-quarter mile race track. Scott Kelly also raced one of his grays against Sheidler's horse; however, Kelly's Irish luck wasn't with him that day. Sheidler's horse won that race as well. Newspaper articles later confirmed Scott Kelly's gray mare was indeed a fast horse, paying him a purse of $500 in one race (*Pueblo Chieftain* November 19, 1868) and $1000 in another (*Pueblo Chieftain* November 17, 1870:)

First race on Saturday 300 yard dash won by Scott Kelly's gray mare. Second was for quarter horses and won by Mr. Davis's horse, 'Blackie' and third race was a 600 yard race won by Joel Roe's horse 'Humpy'. The fourth race was a singe race of 1,000 yards and was won by Scott Kelly's gray mare.

It's hard to know with any degree of certainty what firearms Sheriff Kelly may have carried in the shootout with the Salt Lake City Jim Gang, or during his many other deadly encounters that were soon to follow. But, there does seem to be a consensus of expert opinions among collectors of western firearms in Colorado from the 1860s. Most firearms collectors from the period agree that Sheriff Kelly was likely armed with two black powder revolvers, possibly a long gun, also firing black powder, and definitely a knife; as many gunfights in the west ended in a knife fight. The most popular handguns carried were Colts, of various sizes, one was probably smaller than the other, which would make it easier to carry and more concealable.

Often used was the Colt 1851 Navy Model six-shot "cap and ball" revolver, likely either a .44 or .36 caliber. Wild Bill Hickok preferred the smaller bore .36 which had less of a punch but offered the shooter a more manageable recoil, vital for getting off a well-placed second or third shot. Even though the revolver's cylinder could hold six rounds, the cylinder directly under the hammer was traditionally carried empty to prevent an accidental discharge. Early western revolvers were notorious for accidentally firing or going off half-cocked, especially when the gun was accidentally dropped or the hammer was struck from above. Many cowboys in the West were known to roll up a small piece of paper, along with a two-dollar bill, which they shoved down into the empty chamber. The piece of paper was a will of sorts, indicating who got their saddle and who to notify if they were killed. The money was to pay for their funeral; American cowboys rarely left their debts unpaid.

Another larger revolver that was used by both lawmen and outlaws alike was the 7 ½ inch barrel length Colt Navy and its barrel was probably octagonal and "blued" in color (blued meaning the type of finish, which was black and when held up to the light appeared as the color of dark blue). These old western black powder revolvers required constant cleaning, especially after being fired or exposed to moisture or inclement weather. A popular smaller revolver carried at the time was the 1849 Colt Pocket Revolver .31 "cap and ball" black powder five-shot revolver with a shorter four-inch barrel.

The knife preference of mountain men, scouts, hunters, or trappers in the West during the 19th or 20th Century, was without equal, the Green River belt knife. Green River knives were the best knives made in the west, perhaps in the world, and if there's one thing one didn't skimp on was a good quality knife. Green River knives were usually single-edge, forged from the highest quality steel available, with an average length of about 10 to 12 inches, and it was always carried in a leather sheath. A hilt often separated the handle from the blade, helping the person gripping the knife to keep his hand from slipping down onto the cutting surface if the knife became slippery from blood or if it hit bone.

There were two long guns highly favored at the time and remain so today: a shotgun for close-range or a rifle for long-range. The finest long range black powder rifle in the West in the early 1860s was a Hawkens muzzleloader. With its .53 octagon barrel, a Hawkens was almost unsurpassed with an effective range of 150-200 yards, but in the hands of an experienced shooter, it was accurate at a much further distance, some say well over 300 yards. With Samuel Hawkens opening up a gun shop in 1859 in Denver, Scott Kelly certainly would have had access to Hawkens; however, since he came from eastern Kansas, he could have brought with him a "Beecher's Bible" properly known as a Sharps rifle. These large-bore breach loading rifles, first designed by Christian Sharps in 1848, were well known for their long-range accuracy and rapid rate of fire.

The shotgun or scattergun, if intended for close-quarters fighting, was quite likely a double barrel side by side (SxS) shotgun, smoothbore, more than likely a 12 gauge or possibly a 10-gauge muzzleloading shotgun. When these shotguns were fired the smoke and fire that erupted forth from the burning black powder put up a smoke screen several feet in diameter and the noise was deafening to all and disorienting to those not accustomed to gunfights. Hollis & Sheak, from Birmingham, Alabama, produced shotguns, as well as rifles and pistols from 1849 to 1861. These high-quality firearms are stamped with the name Hollis & Sheak, along with proof marks, on the barrels, and made their way into the American West during Kelly's time as sheriff.

North and South Conflicts in Colorado

There was little doubt to the settlers in the Colorado Territory that law and order were needed and that the conflict between the North and the South back east had followed them to their new home. Reports in newspapers and by travelers along the front range would eventually reach to El Paso County. The November 28, 1861, *Colorado City Journal* ran an announcement asking for five volunteers from Colorado City for Company A 1st Regiment Colorado Volunteers, to be led by Major John Chivington.

On October 1st, 1861, Denver newspapers reported 100 Rebels under the command of Captain Miller had skirmished with Union forces resulting in one death. Two weeks later on October 14, 1861, newspapers reported a confrontation between Union supporters and "secessionists" at Georgia Gulch resulted in one more death. On October 25, 1861, newspapers in the Colorado Territory reported a large Rebel guerrilla force had intercepted and captured a Union wagon train on the Santa Fe Trail along the Cimarron Branch, south of the Arkansas River traveling from Fort Union to Fort Wise.

On October 26, 1861, newspapers in Denver City reported a man named "Heffner" was in the City and had been recruiting local men to help free a southern rebel named McKee and his men from the Denver jail. The same day Chief Justice of the Colorado Territory, B. F. Hall, wrote to President Lincoln concerning the unrest in the Territory and asked the President to send more federal troops. In his letter Chief Justice Hall was also seeking guidance from President Lincoln, also an attorney, on how the new Territory should treat local prisoners; Judge Hall questioned if these men were to be considered common criminals, prisoners of war (POWs), or political detainees? Chief Justice Hall was no doubt referring to the 44 Rebel prisoners captured at Mace's Hole, near Beulah.

On November 28, 1861, *The Colorado City Journal* published Volume 1 Number 18. Under the headlines "The U.S. Prisoners and their Crimes" the article read in parts: "We give below a list of the names of prisoners recently brought into the city. The canon (a sixteen pounder), mentioned before in our column was captured at the location…and hearing that such an instrument of succession argument was waiting to catch a Union "napper," at the above place, (US) Marshall Townsend." *The Colorado City Journal* printed the names of the prisoners:

Columbus W. Asher	Jasper C. Bell
Thaddeus P. Bell	Geo. Booth
James N. Bradley	Alex B. Bradshaw
Hancy Briggs	Abraham C. Brown
Geo. Chamberlin	Thomas Chewning
Harmon R. Clanton	James Cowan
Marion J. Diggs	John S. Easton
Jerome S. Glick	Daniel K. Gunt
Vincent Gray	Nelson Harin
Geo. A. Jackson	Theo. H. Johnson
Robert E. Johnston	Ransford Lawrence
John Marvel	Geo. M. McClosky
Joel McKee	Cornnell Meeks
John S. Mers	Samuel Mers

Wm. L. Mers	William Murry
Anderson Nilson	Wm. M. Nunnelly
Wm. H. Porter	James Reynolds
John Reynolds	Addison F. Stone
Wm. Tipton	J.C. Trotter
John L. Wallace	Andrew J. Wilson
Wm. Winn	John C. Work

The Colorado City Journal newspaper article reported the following:

Forty-four human beings, including Captain McKee, are now in jail awaiting the action of the District Court, charged with treason, misprisoning treason, robbery...God grant that the Chief Justice of this territory who was commissioned by President Lincoln to protect these misguided men may be saved the terrible duty of pronouncing the sentence of death up them all...The secessionists charge that the Chief Justice is hickory – by which they mean undoubtedly that he is heartless and severe. His sentences of Adler and Brown and his permission to Reed to get his wayward boy home show that he is sympathetic and humane. We are firmly convinced, ourself, that he is painfully burdened with is terrible duty in respect to these prisoners. We know he will be as lenient as possible; but who, we ask, wo'd take his place for the next three months?

The biggest challenge for the Chief Justice of the Colorado Territory, and the U.S. Marshall Townsend was what to do with these prisoners once they arrived in Denver. The federal penitentiary in Leavenworth was 600 miles away and the only two forts in Colorado, Fort Garland, and Fort Wise, were hemorrhaging troops headed back east to fight with the north, or the south, and volunteers were desperately being sought across the Territory to back-fill those posts. Old western jails, what few there were, were porous and many underpaid jailers were known to have had southern sympathies. As Confederate Colonel Heffinger's 600 troops, minus the 44 who were in jail, marched south to join up with General Sibley's Texans, the rebels briefly considered attacking Fort Garland. The Fort would have given Sibley's troops a place to gather provisions once they returned to the Colorado Territory to obtain much-needed gold for the Confederacy, and then on to the California coast far to the west.

On November 28, 1861, Denver City newspapers reported that 2nd Lieutenant Joshua S. Travilla, of the Denver Home Guard, had been shot during the night by an unknown assailant. Less than two weeks later, on December 8, 1861, 2nd Lt. Travilla died from his gunshot wound. Tensions in Denver City and within its jail continued to boil as authorities struggled to contain the prisoners. It is not known if Chief Justice Hall ever received a reply from President Lincoln asking how to handle the prisoners. However, by February 27, 1862, the point had become moot; Captain Joel McKee and all the "secessionists" being held in the Denver City jail had escaped, and most made their way south to meet up with General Sibley marching north from Texas.

The concerned citizens of Denver eventually became so upset at the nightly activities of the soldiers from Camp Weld that they established a Police Department to protect the town's citizenry from the "Unruly 1st" until they finally marched out of town on February 22, 1862. Mixed feelings were likely felt by many of Denver's citizens and business owners. The First Volunteer Regiment's orders were to engage with General Sibley's Confederate States Army, who were steadily marching north from Texas towards Santa Fe, New Mexico. The Denver Police Department, no doubt owes its origin to the men of the Unruly 1st—the volunteers of the Colorado 1st Regiment.

Sheriff Kelly also had to handle problems with Southern rebels. A few days after the mass jailbreak in Denver City, a horse was stolen from an El Paso County rancher on Fountain Creek just below present-day Colorado Springs. The rancher described how several men, some mounted and several on foot, forced him to catch and saddle his own horse for the thieves as they waited. The horse thieves made some reference to the horse being confiscated in the name of the Confederacy and there may have been an offer to pay for the horse in Confederate currency, which the rancher was said to have refused.

Captain McKee was able to reconnect with the Confederate Army and became instrumental in helping guide General Sibley and his troops north through the mountains of northern New Mexico. Most, if not all, of the other prisoners, including Marion J. Diggs, had also escaped from jail in Denver, and joined up with Sibley. Diggs saw action during battle at Glorieta Pass, where he was shot in the leg. Captain McKee also fought for the Confederates at Glorieta Pass and at one point he and his men were opposed by Major John M. Chivington's forces as they tried to cross a stream. McKee was heard to have shouted, "If that Dog Chivington comes near I will shoot him." No doubt all soldiers wearing gray and some wearing blue felt the same. The major battle at Glorieta Pass, fought from March 26 to 28. 1862, between the North and South would later be called the Gettysburg of the West. The Northern victory at Glorieta Pass would stop the South from reaching Colorado gold.

On July 17, 1862, the 37th Session of the U.S. Congress passed House Resolution No. 110 which authorized the seizure and confiscation of property owned by suspected 'rebels' in any territory or state under the control of the U.S. government.

Irving Howbert, in his book *Memories of a Lifetime in the Pikes Peak Region*, published in 1925, wrote the following:

Between people from the South who remained in Colorado and those of the North, much bitterness existed. The spirit of war was prevalent here as elsewhere, and there were frequent clashes of a serious nature between the contending factions. During the summer of 1861 recruiting for the First Regiment of Colorado Volunteers was underway at Hamilton. Although I was somewhat undersized and probably would not have been accepted, I was anxious to enlist in this Regiment, but on broaching the subject to my parents, they at once vetoed it, and I had to wait until later for my military experience.

Ironically, Irving Howbert's "military service" would be under the command of John Chivington, in 1864 at a place that would become infamously known as the "Sand Creek Massacre."

The First Regiment of Colorado Volunteers had to have taken special note when in December 1861 General Henry H. Sibley, commanding the Army of New Mexico, issued a proclamation that indicated an intention to claim the New Mexico Territory in the name of the Confederacy. General Sibley's soldiers had captured the fully laden Union storehouses intentionally overflowing with millions of dollars worth of war material and provisions, compliments of former Fort Fillmore's commanding military officers and politicians with southern leanings who envisioned this invasion of the New Mexico Territory coming. Should Sibley's expedition in northern New Mexico succeed, there could be no doubt that the Colorado Territory lay clearly within his sights. How exactly Sheriff Kelly and the other sixteen county sheriffs in Colorado were to respond was unclear.

As 1861 drew to an end, Governor Gilpin had to have felt he had done all he could do to achieve what Lincoln had asked him to do—to make certain the Colorado Territory remains in the Union. This was indeed a noble cause; however, there was one problem: Lincoln didn't give Gilpin any money to accomplish his mission and the Territory didn't have any money either. The Colorado Territory was not even a year old and what little money the federal government had was being spent on urgent war efforts back east. Undeterred, Governor Gilpin began issuing paper "scripts," an IOU of sorts, drawn on credit from the federal government, signed by a Territorial governor, without any authorization.

Most of the Denver merchants readily snatched up Governor Gilpin's signed scripts; "better to have the possibility of getting some money, vs. the certainty of getting no money," they may have thought; besides it gave them a way of showing their patriotism for the Union and support of their new Governor, all while getting paid, someday. Scripts bearing Gilpin's signature totaling $375,000 were frequently exchanged between the merchants in Denver City, becoming its own form of currency, for a short while anyway. When word of Gilpin's innovative solution for funding the needs of the new Colorado Territory reached the Nation's Capital, the Governor was summoned to the White House where he was summarily sacked by the man who had appointed him to the position just the previous year: President Abraham Lincoln.

No doubt combined with many men who had settled in El Paso County returning East to their original homes to fight in the war and with those men remaining with sympathies on either the Northern or the Southern sides, the Sheriff of El Paso County would have been stretched thin trying to cover the large territory he oversaw. Throughout November and December of 1862 several companies of the Colorado 1st Cavalry were stationed in El Paso County for training while waiting to be refitted with horses giving Kelly hope of finding back-up.

Capture of James Clarke

On February 13, 1864, shocking news spread across the Colorado Territory; the U.S. Mint in Denver had been robbed! Technically, it wasn't a robbery, but embezzlement by a young pay clerk employed at the mint. Newspapers stated, "February 13, 1864: Local newspaper report the U.S. Mint in Denver 'robbed' of over $36,817.05 (in gold bars, coins, currency, etc.) by James D. Clarke." James Clarke had, "lit out for parts unknown." Almost as shocking as the "daring robbery" had occurred in the first place was news of who was responsible for the audacious crime; causing Denver City to be, "stirred to its profoundest depths." According to several sources, young Mr. Clarke was said to be a "bright and shining light in religious as well as social circles" who had recently donated money for a pew at the church and the "last man to be suspected of such a disreputable act."

Sheriff Kelly told Dora Foster:

In 1863 a man named Clarke robbed the Denver bank of $70,000. The bank was run by Jim Blaine. Twelve thousand dollars was in gold bars. I captured him (Clarke) at Williams

*Camp on the Fountain about 12 miles from the Arkansas River.
I took him to Colorado City and then on to Denver. My reward
was $2,000.*

Kelly remembered this event and his part in the capture of Clarke, but a few details were clarified when verifying his account. Retired FBI Agent Dale A. Berndt, a fellow historian, and friend of mine, was able to determine "with the admirable help of a librarian" the date was not 1863 but the following year 1864. Kelly considered it a bank robbery but in actuality, it was the U.S. Mint in Denver. Dale also found what Kelly deemed a robbery was actually embezzlement by a Mint employee.

A trip by Dale to the Western History Department of the Denver Public Library revealed two short newspaper reports, including one that read: "February 19, 1864: James Clarke is captured in El Paso County en route to Mexico reportedly to rendezvous with his brother (a Confederate States of America colonel in Mexico) however he only had a little over $29,000 in his possession." Dale Berndt was able to confirm there was a Colonel named Edward Clark (spelled with no "e" at the end) with the 14th Regiment Texas Infantry (Captain Clark's Regiment).

The reward offered for the capture of James D. Clarke was $1,000; however, Sheriff Kelly later claimed his reward was $2,000. It is possible Kelly was paid $1,000 for the capture of James Clarke and another $1,000 for the return of the $29,000; which no doubt pleased and probably surprised officials at the U.S. Mint in Denver, Colorado Territory. The fact Sheriff Kelly turned in $29,000, including gold bars, coins, and currency along with James Clarke alive, is truly a testament to the honesty and integrity of the first lawman in the history of El Paso County. It was reported that of the over $36,817.05 approximately $12,000 was in gold bars, likely extracted from "Pikes Peak Gold," waiting to be minted into U.S. gold coins. There was also a significant number of U.S. Treasury bonds stolen; however, it is unknown if the face value of these bonds was ever included in the total financial loss or recovery.

Often in researching newspapers that recount our past, we find names spelled differently or even reported differently: one reporter might hear the name one way and another report it differently. Multiple people who were used as witnesses might state or spell a name differently as in this case where the name bank manager's name was reported as both Lane and Blaine and Clark's name has been reported as both Clark and Clarke. The amount and what was actually taken were reported differently in various papers too. This was not uncommon in a time when they did not have the technology to "fact find" while reporting. Also, with the inability to spell as notes were taken by hand, errors occurred. Even the U.S. Census reports were filled out by hand and the spelling of names of family members differ along with the memory of when people were born.

The Daily Commonwealth newspaper, Denver City, Colorado (Territory), dated Wednesday, February 17, 1864, printed the article about the affair:

Particulars of the Mint Robbery
A NICE YOUNG MAN!
Furnished Pews in Church

Our City was astounded Monday morning on hearing that the safe of the United States' Branch Mint had been robbed of $34,000 in Treasury Notes, and a bar of gold, worth $3,000, the property of the United States, the greenbacks being those of recently deposited by Geo. W. Brown, Esq., United States Internal Revenue Collector for Colorado Territory.

James D. Clarke, the Pay Clerk of the Mint, and who of course, was entrusted with one of the keys to the safe, came into the building about six o'clock on Saturday evening, passed through the room where Mr. Lane was sitting, saluting him as he did so in his usual cheerful, manner with "Good evening Mr. Lane," and went into the adjoining 'Pay room.' After remaining there a few minutes, he passed out into the hall, through another door, and thence from the building. In all of this, there was nothing unusual, in the least, and of course nothing to arouse suspicion in the mind of Mr. Lane. It was not yet dark, other officers of the mint were still about the building, the night watchman had not yet entered upon his duties. Mr. Clarke had the entire confidence of Mr. Lane to whom he had been most highly recommended as a young man of unblemished character and reputation: of good family in the east and well connected in this city. His conduct had been, so far as Mr. Lane's observation extended, most praiseworthy.

On Monday morning Mr. Clarke was not at his post. It was understood that he had gone into the country to spend the Sabbath. About ten o'clock, the safe was opened, and the reason of his failure to appear at once manifested itself. $37,000 belonging to the United States, had been abstracted, but several bars of gold belonging to private individuals, and several packages of United States' Treasury Notes of small denomination were left.

Suspicion of course fell upon Clarke. It was discovered that a window of the room was propped up with a pencil, and as he had not been in the building since Saturday, it was taken for granted that he had placed the money on the window on Saturday night and after passing outside, had taken it.

It was soon discovered, that on Saturday he had bought a splendid saddle and bridle, with holsters and saddle bags, paying therefore nearly seventy dollars; that at another place he had purchased a splendid pair of pistols for which he had paid two fifty dollar bills; at Smith & Martin's Livery Stable he hired the best ridding horse in the establishment, that he had brought to him and he placed the saddle upon him, with his own hands; that he gave the man who brought the horse around two dollars with which to buy him a pair of gloves and after obtaining these, sent him for a bottle of brandy, to a drug store, and that about *nine o'clock on Saturday evening, he started up F Street at an easy gallop, since which he had not been seen in the city.*

Mr. Lane immediately took steps to overtake him, in which he was heartily seconded by the Military Commander in the District. If the young scamp succeeds in getting away, it will be because he has more accomplices than is now supposed. Although a passably good horseman, it is hardly probable that he is physically capable of running a successful race with the boys of the "First" even with all the advantages of his start. The "boys" can ride two miles to his one, and have the advantage of a thorough knowledge of the country which Clarke cannot have, and with relays of horses as well as of men, if he took the direction of New Mexico, as was supposed, the news of his flight is already two hundred miles in advance of him.

Upon the facts becoming public, there was no lack of collateral evidence of the guilt of the young man. Notwithstanding he had just purchased and handsomely furnished a pew in one of our churches, testimony of his loose morals came in a perfect avalanche. Wine and women had already found him to be a devout worshipper at their shrine; while stories of his losses at play, at the most respectable 'hells' in the city, poured in upon the ear of Mr. Lane, in one continued stream. One gentleman in high official position said, 'I had it upon my tongue's end a half dozen times in my conversation with you, last Saturday to warn you that he had fallen into the clutches of gamblers, but one thing and another prevented, until it passed from my mind; but afterward, I determined to come and tell you of the fact today.' It also came out, that he had on one evening, lost $900 at play, $300 of which he had paid down, settling the balance by giving his note.

For some time, he has been borrowing money, paying large notes of interest therefore, and on Saturday morning, he had made every great exertion to borrow $1,200, as he said, to make *a purchase of cattle. One theory is, that when first induced to play, he won largely for a time, (which is positively said to be the fact.) This furnished him with money with which to indulge his propensities in other directions. Very soon his luck turned. It is the same old story – he borrowed of his friends – then he abstracted from the vaults of the Mint, with the hopes of replacing it before detection – that he knew he could not go longer than the next Monday with being discovered, and that as he failed to borrow the amount, he concluded that he might as well go for a big thing and he went for it.*

This idea receives confirmation from the vest that all the money in the vault was not taken; if others had joined with him, of course they would have taken the other thousands of dollars left behind. Happily, perhaps, for the gamblers of this city, the indignation of the people, which would otherwise fall upon them, is checked by the fact that this is not Clarke's first peccadillos (trivial affair). At least, so it seems, from two letters received by a young man now in jail in this city, from his sister in Pittsburg, Pa., warning him to beware what company he kept; not to associate with bad or wild young men, and cautioning him particularly not to associate with James Clarke, who had left home on account of having committed a forgery, or something of that nature, there.

Five days later, on February 22, 1864, the *Daily Commonwealth* newspaper in Denver City, published this headline and story reporting Sheriff Kelly's capture of Clarke:

THE MINT ROBBERY! CAPTURE OF CLARKE!

He assumes the name 'Jim Jones'. He professes sympathy for Mexico: Claims to be a Lieut. Colonel! He trembles when arrested and confesses all. Enticed into gambling by nice suppers. The excitement of the past week culminated yesterday, on the arrival in town of Mr. Amos Lane, Mr. Crocker, Mr. Kelly, Sheriff of El Paso County, and James D. Clarke, the absconding Pay Clerk of the United States Branch Mint in this city. The party drove up to the mint, in front of which a large, well-dressed and remarkably jocular crowd assembled. None others but employees of the Mint were admitted, and for two hours the crowd continued to increase. At the end of that time, Clarke was taken to his new quarters on Larimer Street. He is very much altered in appearance, through exposure and exhaustion, so that his old acquaintances did not recognize him at first glance. The story of his capture is nearly as follows:

On Tuesday afternoon about five o'clock, Mr. Amos Lane, son of the Superintendent of the Mint, in the company of Mr. Crocker, a freighter, left Denver in a buggy, having heard that a horse answering the description of the one rode by Clarke had been seen at the head of Cherry Creek; the two stopped the night at Mr. Slyer's about fifteen miles from Denver; starting early the next morning, they reached the place where the horse had been seen, but could find no further trace of it. They then concluded to pursue their search, and went on to the lower mill and thence up the Creek. At Kerr's Mill they found that a person answering Clarke's description had been leading a horse and that he had afterward hired Mr. Maine to guide him down to Mexico, and that he had furnished Mr. Maine with money, with which to buy a pony. The stranger had said that he was lost—that he had a brother in the Mexican army whom he wished to join, as he had just received a Lieutenant Colonel's commission—that the reason he had left the main road, was that Col. Chivington had forbid his going.

Shortly after leaving Kerr's Mill, they (Lane and Crocker) met a Mr. Evans who told them that a young man answering Clarke's description had stayed at his camp on Monday night. Mr. Evan's camp is just over the 'Divide' (in El Paso County), where he is herding cattle. Mr. E. had asked him a great many questions, such as 'What made him go armed so heavily?' To this Clarke said he had had use of firearms once before and now he always went prepared for the worst. He also said he had cattle on the Fountain qui Bouille, and that he was hunting some that had strayed. He gave his name as Jim Jones. Of course, Maine helped this story along. Maine appears to be an honest sort of fellow, and probably believed the story of the Mexican Colonelcy. Everybody spoke of him being a man of integrity.

The weather was very cold, snow was falling, and as there were no other stopping places that they could reach that night Mr. Lane concluded to stay over, until morning, at Mr. Crosby's. The weather was clear, but cold, next morning, when the pursuit was renewed before sunrise. A saddle which Mr. C. furnished was put into the buggy, at this point. Thinking they could make better headway, they struck for the old Santa Fe road. By night they reached Wyte's near Cotton's having traveled about sixty miles that Thursday, but heard no additional things.

They had been at Wyte's but a few minutes when Mr. Kelly, Sheriff of El Paso County came in. He had only just heard of the Mint robbery, but had heard of a couple men who had bought a pony, and tried to hire an ox team to bring in some saddles—which were at their camp a few miles away, their ponies having strayed. The next morning, Friday, accompanied by the Sheriff, they started early and struck the trail of their suspicioned individuals, and in two hours came to a little cabin where Clarke and Maine were eating breakfast.

The Sheriff first went into the cabin and laying his hand on Clarke said, 'You are my prisoner,' while Messrs. Crocker and Lane remained outside for a few minutes. When Mr. Lane went in, Clarke was trembling violently, but asked leave to finish breakfast, which consisted of bread, molasses, and a *little bacon. In a few minutes his appetite failed him, and the party, now numbering five persons was enroute for Denver.*

At Cotton's, the Sheriff went off to get a team, and then Clarke began to ask if there were bills out, and if his description was given—what the papers had said about him, &c. It was not, however, until he reached Colorado City, that he saw the Commonwealth, containing a full account of the robbery, which he read through without remark; but upon laying the paper down, he laughingly said—'Well, some of that is true, and some isn't.' What he objected to, was the 'wine and women' portion of the account, and the story about the letter to the prisoner from his sister in Pittsburg; averring that he knew nothing upon which such a story could be based. [A dozen persons have seen these letters, and their genuineness has been doubted.]

He said that he had only commenced gambling about two weeks before, and that up to within twenty-five minutes of the time he went to the Mint, the thought of leaving town had not occurred to him; that he had tried with all his might to borrow money to replace what he had previously abstracted, and then came to the conclusion that it might be much better for him to be proven a big rascal than a little one—that if he got away, he might as well get it all as having nothing. He said that he was sorry Supt. Lane had been deceived in him. He had the key of the safe with him. Sometimes he was thoughtful and gloomy, and at others he would laugh and joke about matters and things in general.

Gen. Lane, the Superintendent, went down to Colorado City last Saturday, but took the Coberly route, while his son and party came by the stage route. The General would, of course, hear the good news at Colorado (City), and was expected home by stage last night.

We are not able to state exactly how much money was

recovered, but the major part of it was in the saddle-bags. Of course, it is easy to trace the amounts he has dispensed of, even if he were not so willing to tell. It was current on the street yesterday, that the bar of gold, worth nearly $3,000, worked through the saddle-bag within a mile of town, and that it has not been recovered; this is all conjecture, we imagine.

The short stages which Clarke made, shows that he had not well calculated his own powers of endurance. Riding horseback is rather a trying business to a raw hand, and Clarke has proved that a guilty conscience and a brandy bottle are not the best companions on a cold night...

The horses, which strayed away from the camp of Clarke and Maine, on Tuesday night, of course the captors, did not stop to hunt for. It seems Clarke became both sick and sore. On the way from the camp, to the cabin where they were arrested, Maine complained about carrying the saddlebags which contained the greenbacks, but Clarke made him do it—as it contained his commission and valuable correspondence.

Maine is temporarily committed to jail, as of course, his testimony is required. A preliminary examination will be held in a day or two, perhaps; but a trial will not be held until the March term of the U.S. District Court.

Most of these particulars we obtained directly from Mr. Lane, who though wearied, very kindly yielded to the natural desire of the public to the particulars. We congratulate him most heartily upon his share in the capture of the thief.

Mr. Amos Lane expresses himself under great obligations to Messrs. Slyer, Evans and Crosby for their kindness, and valuable assistance: also, to his companion, Mr. Crocker, and Sheriff Kelly.

Upon leaving the Mint for the jail, Clarke said to Mr. Eckfeldt, who assisted Deputy U.S. Marshall H. Hunt in conducting him: 'Walk faster, Fredy—there is a good deal more excitement about this thing than I expected—I don't want all these chaps staring at me!' But the crowd kept pace with him, some leading the way, others bringing up the rear, until the jail was reached and he was placed in a felon's cell.

Inside the jail, the interest was about as great as elsewhere, for as soon as the other prisoners were made aware of the accession to their numbers of so distinguished a member of their fraternity, they put their mouths to the diamonds of their cell doors, and in all sorts of phrases, welcomed him with a sort of fiendish jocularity that must have been very gratifying.

'Poor Fool!' say some—'he might have known he would have been caught:' just as if the great punishment would not have been to have escaped the clutches of his pursuers— and to have lived a life of perpetual fear, the great crime forever weighing upon his conscience—starting at his own shadow— frightened at the rustling of a leaf, trembling aghast at the storm; or worse still, as he went on in a career of crime harden-ing his heart to still more serious deeds, and perhaps adding that of murder to the catalogue.

But who can measure the anguish of the mad youth who plunges headlong into a career of crime—who can imagine the full terror of the wail of the soul which, self-affrighted at its own falls, cries inwardly 'Lost! Lost!' Young men of Denver! Think of it! Which road are you travelling?
Remember Jim Clarke.

While James Clarke was being held in the Denver jail, he managed to escape—twice. The first time he was recaptured by U.S. Marshall Farnum at a stage stop on the overland stage route in the mountains northwest of Denver City, near La Porte, Colorado. After several months, Clarke escaped from jail in Denver a second time; however, this time he was never recaptured. Rumors on the streets of Denver City were said to believe Clarke was aided in one or both of his escapes by the Reynolds Gang. The Reynolds brothers, from Texas, had been authorized by Confederate Army's Brigadier General Douglas Cooper by late spring of 1864 to go behind enemy lines in Colorado to begin raiding.

Clarke had spent a lot of money on the expensive saddle, pistols, holster, and other items as he was preparing to leave Denver City. It certainly is possible he may have also paid off some of his gambling debts before leaving town or paid someone who might have aided in his escape; however, it seems somewhat unlikely James Clarke could have spent nearly $8,000, the difference between the amount stolen and what was found on him when he was arrested, in less than a week. When he left Denver he traveled through Russellville a well-known Confederate recruiting and training camp.

The possibility exists that the exact amount of missing gold was not made public; other than the one gold bar worth $3,000 that may have "fallen through the saddlebags," gold bars are quite heavy after all. Sheriff Kelly later said that $12,000 of the missing money was in gold, so perhaps there may have been four gold bars stolen. It was found that some gold bars were left inside the safe in plain view that belonged to private individuals, so there remains some speculation that an audit accounting for precisely what was taken, what was left in the safe, and what was recovered during Clarke's arrest may not have been as precise as one might have expected. The speculation Clarke buried some gold seems consistent with the KGC modus operandi.

One interesting side story is the questions that arise regarding the escaped James Clarke and that of a Jim Clark. It too could be a story of the fine line between law and outlaw, like other lawmen of the American West, including Kelly. Although he may not be the same man; the similarities between James D. Clarke and a Jim Clark, who became the Marshall of Telluride, Colorado, seem almost too striking to readily dismiss. Jim Clark was believed to have been born around 1841 which would have made him about 23 years of age when the robbery occurred at the U.S. Mint in Denver, City, Colorado Territory. Jim Clark was born in Clay County Missouri. His father's last name was Cummings, but his real dad had died when Jim was too young to remember him. Jim's mother remarried another man whose last name was Clark, who became Jim's stepfather and Jim assumed his last name. When Jim was a teenager, he and another local boy had stolen his stepfather's mule and took off on an adventure that led them to San Antonio, Texas. There they stole $1,400 from a rancher before returning to Missouri. Not surprisingly Clark's stepfather didn't exactly welcome Jim back into his home with open arms upon his return.

The family eventually moved to Jackson County, Missouri, where Jim's mother often took in boarders as a way of earning extra income. One of their borders was William Clarke Quantrill, who had initially come to the area to teach school. William Clarke (spelled with an "e") Quantrill and the Clarks became good friends and Jim looked up to and respected William Quantrill. As violence between the Kansas "Jayhawkers" and the Missouri "Border Ruffians" escalated William Quantrill recruited a band of Rebel guerrilla fighters which rapidly grew to about 350 men. When Jim Clark was roughly eighteen years old, about 1859-1860, he joined Quantrill's Raiders who were successful in harassing Union forces and soon became very adept at guerrilla warfare. Jim Clark eventually learned to handle a gun and after demonstrating his fearlessness, became one of Quantrill's most trusted leaders. Quantrill was known as one of the principal leaders of the KGC.

In August of 1863, Quantrill's Raiders conducted a revenge raid on Lawrence, Kansas, which became known as the Lawrence Massacre. It is not known for certain; however, it may be assumed that Jim Clark was with still riding with William Clarke Quantrill and "Bloody Bill" Anderson and if so, he may have participated in the Lawrence Massacre. Senior Confederate leadership immediately became appalled at the sheer violence Quantrill's Raiders demonstrated in killing somewhere between 185-200 unarmed men and boys, executing nearly every single male occupant of the town. The Confederate States soon began distancing themselves from William Quantrill and his raiders.

It is not known precisely when, or where, but at some point, the leadership of KGC began to realize the likelihood of the South winning the war was no longer realistic. Their focus shifted from succeeding from the Union to robbing from the North and burying caches of gold and arms with which to launch a second Civil War. The U.S. Mint in Denver had to have made a tempting target. The Mint had just opened for business, in April 1863, having acquired the building and equipment from investment firm Clark, Gruber and Company headquartered in Leavenworth, Kansas. Was Jim Clark and James D. Clarke the same person? It is not known what date James D. Clarke first went to work as a pay clerk for the U.S. Mint in Denver City; however, it had only been opened for business a few months before the Lawrence Massacre.

After the Civil War ended, Jim Clark joined up with the James and Younger brothers, who had also ridden with Quantrill's Raiders and went on to rob countless banks, trains, and stagecoaches. Both the James and Younger brothers belonged to slave-owning families with deep ties to the South. Several sources suggest the outlaw Jesse (Woodson) James was a confirmed member of the KGC. Jim Clark eventually separated from the James-Younger Gang and returned to Colorado where he became a miner in Leadville. Clark was suspected of being involved in a number of hold-ups and other crimes during the years in the late 1870s to mid-1880 that he spent in Leadville.

In 1887 Jim Clark drifted into Telluride, Colorado, where he took a job digging a ditch and settled into a small cabin where he lived. At the time Telluride was a lawless frontier mining town and the only marshal was afraid to take on the drunken ruffians who shot up the town every night. One day Jim Clark approached the town mayor and convinced the mayor to appoint him deputy marshal, and said he would clean up the town. The mayor agreed and that night Clark physically confronted the rowdy cowboys, miners, and other ruffians, and the town slept peacefully for the first time in months. The next day the mayor made Jim Clark the permanent town marshal.

Before long rumors spread that Jim Clark was continuing his lawless ways, he was just doing it outside of the city limits. Several robbery victims and witnesses believed Clark was committing these crimes while wearing a disguise. Other townsfolk suspect Clark of tipping off other robbers when gold and silver shipments were expected, then get a percentage of the proceeds. On June 24, 1889, Butch Cassidy and his gang robbed the San Miguel County Bank in Telluride and rode away with a large sum of money. Jim Clark later admitted to being paid $2,200 for being conveniently out of town that day.

Despite suspicions of his unlawful behavior, Jim Clark managed to remain the town's Marshal for several years and keep the streets of Telluride quiet at night. He was known to have helped Sheriff Cyrus Wells "Doc" Shores of Gunnison capture cattle rustlers near Gunnison and they became close friends. Clark was recognized for being generous in helping the town's needy and elderly, helping out with chores, repairing their shacks, and lending money to destitute families. Eventually, the Telluride town council decided they needed to act on all the rumors about Clark's lawlessness, and after finding a suitable replacement, fired Jim Clark as their town marshal. Clark was furious; he threatened retaliation and even beat up his replacement one night on the street. Town officials wanted him gone.

Around midnight on August 5, 1895, at about midnight, Jim Clark was walking down Main Street with another man, known only as "Mexican Sam," when Clark was shot once in the chest. The bullet severed an artery before exiting his back. Jim Clark died a short time later on August 6, 1895; he was fifty-four years of age. Rumor had it a member of the town council was behind his death. Like Sheriff Kelly, Jim Clark was a lifelong bachelor and had no family in the Telluride area. When Jim Clark was buried the whole town turned out to attend his funeral. He is buried in the Lone Tree Cemetery, in Telluride, Colorado, beneath a white grave marker that reads, "James Clark CSA."

Indian Wars 1864

During Kelly's term as Sheriff, troubles between the Indians and pioneers were starting to become more prevalent, culminating with a battle fought at Sand Creek. Settlers of the time felt the battle was retribution for killings of frontier families and thefts of cattle and horses done by Indians. Some of the most high-profile victims of this period, were Nathan Ward Hungate, his beautiful twenty-five-year-old wife Ellen, and their two daughters Laura (age two) and little five-month-old Florence. This small family was brutally murdered in June 1864 and their deaths served as a catalyst to finally raise the additional 100-day troops required to field the 3rd Colorado Regimental Cavalry who attacked Black Kettle's camp at Sand Creek in November 1864. Still controversial today among historians, the battle at Sand Creek in November of 1864, also known as the Sand Creek Massacre, occurred during Kelly's term as Sheriff. Later, when asked about his profession, Kelly said that among jobs such as builder, teamster, sheriff, and rancher, he was an Indian fighter.

Before the spring of 1864 travelers on the roads to Denver did not experience open hostilities with the Plains Indians, but that was about to change. These skirmishes were called the Indian Wars of 1864 and

1868; however, the early El Paso County pioneers who lived through them would say the Indian Wars began in 1864 and ended in 1869, with peaks of violence in 1864 and 1868. These pioneers who fought in the Indian Wars in the Colorado Territory would also have said they weren't Indian Wars but a Cheyenne War, although other tribes clearly participated, including the Arapaho and Sioux, along with bands from the Kiowa, Lakota, Comanche and Apache tribes.

During this time Sheriff Kelly made a trip to Denver City where he purchased repeating rifles which he distributed to citizens who were forted up at various locations across the county. It was Kelly's responsibility to get El Paso County ready if any Indian problems arose in his area. Sheriff Kelly later submitted a bill to the El Paso County Commissioners, who reimbursed Kelly for the purchase of these firearms. On June 24, 1864, Governor John Evans issued a proclamation to the "friendly Indians of the plains," directing them to go to designated "places of safety." For the Southern Cheyenne and Arapaho that designated place of safety was Fort Lyon (formerly Bent's New Fort then Fort Wise). Two weeks later on August 11, 1864, Governor Evans issued a second proclamation, this one authorizing all Colorado citizens, "to kill and destroy enemies of the country, wherever they may be found, all such hostile Indians...Parties furnishing their own horses will receive 40¢ per day, and rations for the same while in service. The Company will also be entitled to all horses and plunder taken from the Indians."

In his book, *Memories of a Lifetime in the Pike's Peak Region*, Irving Howbert reports how times were changing with Indians other than the local Ute Indians that were in El Paso County:

The plains Indians were tall, athletic people while the Utes were directly the opposite, being short and heavy set. The Ute language is in no wise related to that of any of the Indians of the plains, excepting the Comanches, who are a kindred people. The Cheyennes and Arapahoes were virtual interlopers in this region. Both tribes were of the Algonquin stock whose original home was in the New England States and southern Canada. When first heard about in 1750, the Cheyenne Indians were located in northern Minnesota. In 1790, they were living on the Missouri River near the mouth of the Cheyenne. A little later they moved west into the Black Hills, having been driven there by the Sioux. Here they were joined by the Arapahoes and from that time on the two tribes were bound together by the closest relations. They lived in the same villages and roamed in company over the great plains.

Early settlers to the Colorado Territory who knew the land and the people of these tribes could feel change in the air; like a spring storm rising on the horizon stirring the tall yellow buffalo grass on the prairie. Change was coming in the spring of 1864. The men of these Indian tribes were no longer interested in trading their thick buffalo robes for anything other than rifles and ammunition. Irving Howbert offers a rare primary source account of how the Indian troubles of 1864 began in his book *Indians of the Pike's Peak Region*, first published in 1914:

At the time the hostilities began, I was little more than eighteen years old, and as fond of excitement and adventure as boys at that age usually are. I had a part in many of the occurrences which I shall mention, and was personally familiar with the details of most of the others.

Until 1864, every spring after the white settlers came into this region, war-parties of Cheyenne, Arapahoe, and Sioux would come trailing in from the plains, pass through Colorado City, stopping long enough to beg for food from the families living near the line of their march and then go on to the soda springs; here they would tarry long enough to make an offering to the Great Spirit who was supposed to be manifested in the bubbling waters, and then follow, in single file, up the Ute Pass trail into the South Park, where they would scout around until they had found a band of Ute. If they succeeded in surprising the latter, they would probably come back with a lot of extra ponies and sometimes with captured squaws and children, in which case they would exhibit a jubilant air; but at other times on their return, they would present such a dejected appearance that one could readily surmise that they had suffered defeat. These annual visits were discontinued after the tribes became involved in warfare with the whites.

About the 20th of June, 1864, word reached Colorado City that a day or two previously, the Hungate family, living on Running Creek about forty miles northeast of Colorado City, had been murdered by the Indians. The father and mother had been shot down and mutilated with horrible brutality, and the children who had tried to escape had been pursued and killed, so that not one of the family were left alive. This news made the people of Colorado City and the settlers along the Fountain and on the Divide, very uneasy, and of course, after that, they were constantly on the lookout, not knowing where the savages might next appear.

Irving Howbert mentions in his writing that many of the Ute Nation spent the winter of 1864-1865 camped peacefully along Fountain Creek on the southern edge of Colorado City. Sheriff Kelly was probably not the only El Paso County resident happy to see 1864 come to an end; unfortunately, 1865 wasn't going to be much better. El Paso County resident, J.B. Simms painted an alluring picture of how 1864 may have drawn to a close as the early pioneers of El Paso County gathered in Colorado City to celebrate Christmas and perhaps ponder what the New Year might bring:

When the wild plains Indians were hostile...with the nation in the throes of a great rebellion, the eastern border of Kansas, through which the emigrants to the Pikes Peak region must pass, was aflame with fire and steel. And yet it seems to me, people were more happier in Colorado City in the early days than now. At Christmas times we had shooting matches, a horse race or two, plenty of Tom and Jerry (a common name during the Civil War for alcohol), and usually wound up the day with a dance at the Anway fort and a supper at Smith and Baird's hotel. Often half dozen families would arrange a friendly dinner at some neighbor's house, and the hotel men would make a big dinner and invite the ranchmen to come in and enjoy the festivities. The pious people who were adverse to horse racing would generally pitch horseshoes and sometimes end the day in a big game of draw poker. There was not much money in circulation, and the betting on a horse race was commonly a sack of flour, a side of bacon or a shotgun. No, we never hung the horse thieves on Christmas. Those festivities were held until the new-year, so as to start the community off with good resolutions.

Aftermath of Civil War and the Wild West

A s the Civil War ended, thousands of men, especially from the southern states, didn't have a home in which to return. Many who came west were violent and law enforcement in the west faced a new level of lawlessness.

On May 5, 1865, what was believed to be the first train robbery in America occurred near North Bend, Ohio. A group of well-organized outlaws derailed a westbound train bound for St. Louis, Missouri, and robbed the train and its passengers before making their escape. The outlaws, some speculated afterward, were Confederate bushwhackers perhaps even members of the KGC. Since the James-Younger Gang was centered in central Missouri, the names of the James brothers (Jesse and his brother Frank) and the Younger brothers (Cole, Jim, John, and Bob) have been included among the list of possible suspects. The James-Younger Gang was well-known for their willingness to take on high-risk, high-yield targets for robberies; including banks, stagecoaches, and trains. Both the James and Younger brothers belonged to slave-holding families with deep ties to the South.

On July 21, 1865, the first recognized Western gunfight occurred when a former Union soldier Wild Bill Hickok shot and killed Dave

Tutt during a "quick draw dual" in the market square of Springfield, Missouri. Dave Tutt was a former Confederate officer. He and Hickok were initially friends, until falling out over a gambling dispute; Hickok allegedly owed Tutt a previous gambling debt. Some historians claim the first man killed in a gunfight with Hickok was David McCanles, who was allegedly threatening the Rock Creek Station Manager in Fairbury, Nebraska when he was shot and killed in 1861. There is some dispute as to who actually killed McCanles, as two other men were arrested along with Hickok for murder. All three men were later acquitted when it was decided they acted in self-defense. Wild Bill Hickok would go on to become a legendary gunfighter and gambler, as well as a lawman.

In the aftermath of Sand Creek, the decision to allow the Cheyenne or Arapaho to return to their former home on the Reserve east of El Paso County and north of the Arkansas River was simply not a concession the government and the military were willing to make. The railroads were bringing new homesteaders, and towns renewed commerce along the Santa Fe Trail, was on its way. The Cheyenne would have to go to Indian Country. Like many other tribes already relocated to the Reservations in present-day Oklahoma, some of the Cheyenne would go peacefully, many would go only after being escorted by armed soldiers, a few would try to assimilate or blend into the white man's culture, some would not go at all, resisting relocation until their last breath.

Irving Howbert writes in *Indians of the Pikes Peak Region*:

In the winter of 1865-1866, a large body of Ute Indians camped for several months on the south side of the Fountain (Creek), opposite Colorado City. On departing in the spring, they abandoned a squaw who had broken a leg, leaving her in a rudely constructed tent or tepee. Had not the women of Colorado City taken her in charge she would have starved. After the Indians left, she was moved into a log cabin in Colorado City and provide with all she need until her death, which occurred a few months later.

The Ute seemed to think nothing of this heartless act, and even the abandoned squaw did not seem to resent it. It was a very common occurrence for the Indians of most of the tribes to abandon the aged and disable, as in moving around, they did not wish to be burdened with those who were incapable of taking care of themselves.

Big Tooth Jim

Sheriff Kelly completed his four-year term in 1866 and disregarded the encouragement of many of his personal friends and citizens to run for a second term in office. Kelly may have told his friends he hadn't come to the Pikes Peak Region to become a lawman; what he did not tell them was that he was running from the law. There was a lot of attention focused on people in elected office, especially in a growing county at the heart of the Colorado Territory. But being in public office wasn't in Kelly's plan, his dreams were to use his skills as a carpenter and stonemason, to build himself a nice ranch to raise many cattle and his prized gray horses and perhaps someday raise a family.

Reminding people he had his horse shot out from under him twice, Rankin Scott Kelly said he'd, "had enough", then retired from law enforcement and handed the Sheriff's Office over to Burt Myers, a Colorado City merchant. President Abraham Lincoln was inaugurated for his second term on March 4, 1866, so there is a possibility Bert Myers was sworn in as El Paso County Sheriff on March 4, 1866. Kelly had been appointed El Paso County's first Sheriff in 1861 and then elected to a four-year term the following year, so he had actually served five years as the Sheriff. However, El Paso County's second Sheriff, Bert Myers, would only last three days.

Burt Myers had no known prior law enforcement experience; however, he did have a good horse and had bought himself a new handgun. Myers had also watched Sheriff Kelly ride off in pursuit of countless desperadoes and hostile Indians and he always seemed to come back no worse for wear. On Sheriff Myers' third day on the job, the Big Tooth Jim Gang rode into El Paso County. Big Tooth Jim was a huge man, 6 feet 4 inches, 240 pounds, and big ears that stuck straight out from his head. He had two enormous front teeth that protruded outward from his lips, resembling tusks. He was known to wear a metal plate, which hung around his neck with a leather strap, covering his chest, which he used as a bullet-resistant vest. The Native Americans told Sheriff Kelly that Big Tooth Jim was a man who could never be killed.

The two members of Big Tooth Jim's murderous gang riding with him were described by Sheriff Kelly as a "Mexican and half-breed Negro." This outlaw gang had become known as the Terror of the Rockies, for they alone were believed to be responsible for at least 35 murders, including the rape and murder of two young Mexican girls, who were sisters. Most of the male victims had been robbed, their livestock shot, and several of the men had also been tied up and tortured, simply out of meanness. Shortly after Sheriff Myers rode out to arrest the Big Tooth Jim Gang, the Sheriff was seen walking back into Colorado City; the outlaws had stolen the Sheriff's horse and his new gun. Burt Myers took off the Sheriff's badge and resigned acknowledging, "Those fellas were too rough for me."

Someone went to fetch Scott Kelly, to tell him about the Big Tooth Jim Gang being in the County, but he reminded them he was no longer Sheriff. Then they told Kelly that Bert had quit and the gang had stolen Bert's horse and his new gun. Reluctantly, Scott Kelly put down his hammer, pinned on the Sheriff's badge, and prepared for another manhunt; this one would take him deep into the New Mexico Territory, a trip covering well over five hundred miles. Big Tooth Jim and his gang of desperadoes were pure evil on horseback and were terrifying the citizens of the Pikes Peak Region. Although we don't know exactly where or when Kelly's shootout with the Big Tooth Jim Gang occurred, we do know it was in the New Mexico Territory. Scott Kelly shared a few of the details with Dora Foster during his interview in 1913:

The last that was heard of Jim he was going down towards the Mexico line, killing and robbing as he went. I'm going after him this week. I'll take Dan Gassenger with me. He is a sure shot and reliable and will be all the help I'll need. We came home by easy stages but going down we did not let the grass grow under our feet, for the ranchers all along the way kept telling us that he was about a day ahead of us. Reports showed he had killed about 35 men besides several women and children, two young girls 12 and 14 years old. Maxwell of the Maxwell Grants begged us to turn back, saying no man ever went out after that fellow and came back alive. But I explained that I was so familiar with that part of the country that I was the one to go after him. He had tied up several men he had robbed and then beaten them to death and then driven off their cattle and horses. He had with him a half-breed Negro and a Mexican.

I had guessed that Jim would camp near a certain spring and so that night we crept to within nearly 50 feet of their camp and waited there in the bright moonlight for daylight. It gave us a chance to get pretty nervous. We waited there about three hours. We could see the three of them rolled in their blankets beside their fire. I was to take Jim while Dan took care of the other two.

Just as the sun rose they woke. Dan was to fire when I counted three and we were both to pick off our men. We reloaded our guns fearing to trust the bullets that had been in our guns all night. The Negro got up first and went towards the horse that was picketed nearby; the Mexican started to make a fire and just as the big fellow threw up his arms and tossed back his blanket, I counted three, took aim, and fired, holding my gun tight, tight against my shoulder. I aimed at the spot just between his shoulders. I got him just there where I had aimed and he rolled over to one side and fell over dead.

Dan's bullets had gone thru the Negro's heart and thru the Mexican's eye.

We hardly dared to go to them, lying just as they fell, but we finally did. Jim's steel plate, which we found was lined with rubber, was tied to his saddle near his bed. Evidently not having been worn for several days, feeling safe I presume in that part of the country. He had nearly $2,000 on his person.

After looking over their good supply of grub we helped ourselves to much of it, especially the bacon, as our own supply was getting low. Then we rolled all three of them over into a little arroyo where there was a tiny spring.

Coming back we stopped at several places to return to those who had not been killed some of the money that had been taken from them.

Dora Foster made note of Sheriff Kelly's philosophy—"You learned to shoot first or get shot."

Photograph of Kelly taken in 1913 while he was working at the Myron Stratton Home. Courtesy, Pioneer Museum.

RANKIN SCOTT KELLY
1868 –1913 THE LATER YEARS

One change that was taking place across eastern Kansas, the Colorado Territory, and Nebraska was the transference of military leadership to a post-Civil War structure to more effectively confront the growing Indian raids on the plains. Brevet Major General George Armstrong Custer became Lieutenant Colonel Custer, although he was allowed the privilege of retaining the title of General when he assumed field command of the 7th Cavalry. By early 1867 Custer had assembled his officers and recruits and prepared them for their new mission; protecting the roads through the newly formed states of Kansas and Nebraska into the Colorado Territory. General Winfield Scott Hancock assumed command of the Department of the Missouri, which also included Kansas and the Colorado Territory. Kelly, no longer Sheriff, would continue to be an Indian Fighter.

Scott Kelly—Indian Fighter

On January 8, 1867, African-American men were granted the right to vote in the District of Columbia, women of any color would have to wait another half-century to have the right to vote in national elections. In the mid-nineteenth century, the Territories out West could each decide if they wanted to extend the right to vote to women; the Wyoming Territory granted women the right to vote in 1869. On March 1, 1867. Nebraska became the 37th state admitted into the Union. The Colorado Territory would wait almost another decade before adding the 38th star to the American flag.

On March 30, 1867, the United States purchased the land that became Alaska from Alexander II of Russia for $7.2 million, a cost of about two cents per acre. The news media thought the acquisition foolhardy, referring to this purchase as "Seward's Folly," since Secretary of State William H. Seward was one of the strongest proponents for the acquisition. The cost was less than half of what the U.S. had paid for the Louisiana Purchase in 1803. Eventually, the fourth major gold rush in American history would begin in Alaska, but first silver would become king in Colorado, and miners and businessmen would again flock to the Rocky Mountains to seek their fortunes, including Rankin Scott Kelly.

The history of the Colorado Territory often describes two Indian Wars; the first in 1864 the second in 1868. The first was during Kelly's term as Sheriff, and the second after he had left office, and by that time Kelly considered himself an experienced Indian fighter. For the early pioneers, and men like Sheriff Kelly who fought in and lived through the Cheyenne Indian Wars (1864-1869), their reality was one of one long continual Indian War. The most violent years, in terms of non-Indian fatalities, were 1864 and again in 1868; resulting in at least 6 cavalry and 79 civilian deaths within just a few months in 1868.

Some high-profile victims of the Cheyenne War in 1868, were thirty-one-year-old Henrietta Dietermann and her five-year-old son John. Kelly was no longer serving as El Paso County Sheriff on August 27, 1868 when Henrietta and John were brutally murdered by a band of 20 Cheyenne, Arapaho, and Sioux Indians on Cherokee Creek (15 miles northeast of El Paso County). As was the case with the Hungate murders of 1864, the Dietermanns were killed just north of the El Paso County line, in Douglas County. The Hungate family had been brutally murdered by hostile Indians, and their home, located along Box Elder Creek about thirty miles southeast of Denver City, was burned to the ground. When four years later, Cheyenne and Arapaho Indians raided the Dietermann homestead, on Comanche Creek, about six miles from the small settlement of Kiowa, this horrific event would serve as the catalyst to end the Cheyenne Wars.

Jeff Broome's well research book, *Cheyenne War, Indian Raids on the Roads to Denver 1864-1869*, reports the case of the Dietermann's as follows:

> *They (Cheyenne and Arapaho) passed through Colorado City and were sullen in their demeanor, but showed papers from the recent Medicine Lodge Treaty which said they were friendly and should not be molested. They indicated that they were going to fight the Ute. Shortly after that they found their enemy in South Park, near present-day Hartsell, and killed six warriors, two or*

three women, as well as taking a young Ute boy captive. It was returning from this violent foray that Colorado citizens suffered. The Pueblo Chieftain later reported that 75-100 Arapaho under Little Chief came into the Fountain Valley and Colorado City. They were all dressed in war paint and were armed with 100 arrows to each warrior. Announcing they were going into the mountains to fight the Ute, it was later believed that in fact they went up there to rendezvous with another war party and made their plan to attack the Colorado settlements.

Upon arriving back at the end of August they divided into a war party that raided and killed around Colorado City and Fountain, and another war party that went up Monument Creek and into the Bijou Basin…on Comanche Creek, things turned deadly. Apollinaris Dietermann had only lived on Comanche Creek two months, having moved there on June 19 (1868). He earlier had lived on Plum Creek, just north of present-day Castle Rock, from 1862 to 1868, where he operated a hotel, bought and sold cattle and made and sold butter. He was married to 31-year old Henrietta and had a young family; John, who was five, and three-year-old Henrietta, 'Hattie.' Mrs. Dietemann was in her third trimester with her third pregnancy when her life ended on this day.

The Dietemanns had recently sold their business on Plum Creek and moved to Comanche Creek where Apollinaris intended to expand his cattle business. He had sold 300 head of cattle when he sold his ranch and hotel in Castle Rock and brought almost $8,000 to Comanche Creek, intending to purchase new cattle from Arkansas once the family got settled at their new home.

While Apollinaris Dietemann was away from the ranch, his sister Maria, describes what happened:

On Tuesday morning about eight o'clock, the 25th of August, 1868, about twenty-five or thirty Indians came right near our houses, with a herd of horse that they had stolen all over the country; and one of the Indians came up to the house and took two horses that were picketed in front of the house, one of which was my brother's (Apollinaris) and the other A. Schindelholz's, and they took all the horses, about seven or eight in number, that were grazing near the house; and two mares and a colt, belonging to my brother, were taken at that time. I saw the Indians drive them off. I know that they were Indians, and the people told me that they were Cheyenne and Arapahoe Indians. After they had the horses away we got frightened and thought it wasn't safe there, and my brother's wife wanted to go away to some neighbors, and those neighbors were ten miles away; so we took all the valuables along that we had in the house that we could carry, and my brother's wife and children and the two hired men, Benedict Marki and Mr. Lawrence, and myself, started up the creek to the nearest neighbor, which was about ten miles. It must have been about nine o'clock when we started; as we was about half the way we seen five or six horses grazing in a gulch, and one of the hired men (Lawrence) wanted to go and take one of those horses and ride over to Kiowa to tell the people we were in trouble, but as we neared the horses some Indians came out of the ravine and shot at us, about five or six in number, and they commenced to shoot at us and we commenced to run, and my brother's wife wasn't able to run, and the Indians overtook her and shot her, killed her and scalped her, and the little boy (John) I had hold of with my hand, but he run towards his mother, as he thought he was safer with her, and they took a hold of him and killed him…The balance of us turned our course and went to Middle Kiowa (today's Kiowa Creek). All of the white people in that neighborhood was together there at Middle Kiowa, as it was safer, and we stayed there until all the trouble was over and we knew the Indians were gone. I saw them shoot my sister-in-law with a revolver, in the breast, and they shot the boy with arrows, and one of them took a hold of him and twisted his neck. This occurred about ten o'clock. After we was at Middle Kiowa about two or three hours my brother came from Denver and A. Schindelholz, also, and about half a dozen of the men went with him to hunt the remains, which they found at the place we left them, and the next day they fetched them in to Denver to be buried.

The August 27, 1868 edition of the *Rocky Mountain News* picked up from there:

Last evening about seven o'clock a team came into town bringing the remains of Henrietta Dietermann [sic] and her boy, the persons spoken of yesterday as having been captured, the latter about five years old, killed by the Indians on Comanche Creek, Tuesday. The boy had been shot several times and his neck broken, the woman had been shot through the body, outraged, stabbed, and scalped. Decomposition had set in and the sight was horrible. They were killed near their house, Mr. Dietermann [sic] being absent. A man who was about to marry Mr. Dietermann's sister, his said sister, and a daughter of the Dietermanns considerably older than the murdered boy, were at the house at the time, but escaped. About thirty Indians came after the man who brought away the bodies Tuesday night, but he succeeded in getting into the station safely. The remains were taken to an empty house in front of the Tremont House, where for an hour or two people came and viewed them.

Although the Civil War had ended there were still plenty of other newsworthy events to report early in 1868. What was on the minds of all the early settlers in the Colorado Territory was the alarming increase in Indian raids and what their new government was going to do to protect them from adding their skeletal remains to those already scattered across the eastern plains.

On April 29, 1868, General William Tecumseh Sherman, General Grant's most trusted Union General during the Civil War, brokered the Treaty of Fort Laramie (1868) between the U.S. Government and the Plains Indians. The Treaty once again reduced the land size of the Cheyenne and Arapaho Reservations, which had once bordered El Paso and Pueblo Counties to the east and Douglas County to the south and extended to the Kansas border. Other than redrawing the boundaries, the second Fort Laramie treaty would have little more effect than the first Treaty of Fort Laramie in 1851, in guaranteeing protection for the Territory's early settlers who were intent on establishing homesteads on what used to be tribal lands. The most desirable land, coveted by both the homesteaders and Plains Indians, was of course any land that held scarce surface water, such as creeks, tributaries, or springs, especially if this land was destined to be used to build the supporting infrastructure for the coming railroads, which the Indians called the Iron Horse.

By 1868 four competing railroads, the Union Pacific, Kansas Pacific, Atchison Topeka, and the Santa Fe, and soon a fifth, General Palmer's Denver and Rio Grande, would be racing to complete what would eventually become a steel noose that would completely encircle the Dog Soldier's territory. When the Union Pacific and the Kansas Pacific railroads began surveying the route through the heart of this territory, their battle leader, Roman Nose, issued a stern warning to the U.S. Army, "If you build a railroad line through my land you will be my enemy for life." Roman Nose would prove true to be a man of his word. Disregarding his stern warning, the East Division of the Union Pacific extended westward from Kansas City, traced the Smoky Hill Creek, then angled northwest following the Smoky Hill Trail to Denver City, cutting directly across the upper corner of what was just two years previous, the Cheyenne and Arapaho Indian Reserve, bordering El Paso County on the east.

Along the Douglas County border in northern El Paso County several forts were also built, in addition another fortified stone enclosure was built south of Palmer Lake (marked today by a stone monument with a plaque listing the names of the families who forted up at this location). Several rural El Paso County residents also forted up at Scott Kelly's ranch on Fountain Creek (east of I25 south of Lake Avenue, where the present-day Shriners' Mule Barn is located). In Colorado City, most citizens were forting up at the Anway Hotel, as they had done in 1864. Henry Templeton had purchased the two-story Anway Hotel in 1863 from Harvey Anway. The property maintained its original name, the Anway Hotel, and today is located at 2818 W. Pikes Peak Avenue. The men fortified the exterior of the hotel using timbers erected upright. While the women brought their children into the hotel to spend the night, most of the men remained outside, riding shifts as lookouts, while their families spent restless nights forted up inside.

David Spielman had moved to El Paso County prior to the 1868 Indian uprising and was living with his family on a ranch along Monument Creek, north of where the Van Briggle Pottery Building had been built (today part of the Colorado College campus). Spielman wrote an article, which he titled, "Trouble with Indians." He described the 1968 Cheyenne Wars this way:

> *It was right after the harvest. On account of many Indian scares that had amounted to nothing, I had become careless; was sick and tired of it. The continued reports about Indians made my wife uneasy, and she said, 'If you are determined to stay on the ranch, let me move over to Colorado City and you can stay here and take care of things.' I said, 'All right.'*
>
> *At that time David Wright was a partner of mine. I told him to yoke up the oxen and take the family to Colorado City, where there was a fort. That morning a herder by the name of Smith, with Johnny Stone, was herding my cattle and some belonging to neighbors. I told the boys they had better keep the cattle on the west side of the Monument in the gulch, as there might be Indians around. I then went to see Mr. and Mrs.*

Everhart, who lived just west of the Rio Grande bridge over the Monument, just above the passenger depot in Colorado Spring, and I talked with Mr. Everhart about the Indians and told him it would be safer for his son, Charlie Everhart, to take his cattle to where mine were and let the three boys take care of them together.

He said he had heard so much about the Indians that he was getting tired of it and didn't want to hear any more about it. I went home, and after Wright had gone to Colorado City with the last load, I lay down in my cabin on a lounge behind the door with a New York Tribune in my hands and soon went fast asleep with the paper over my face. I had lain there probably an hour when I heard a racket at the door; I jumped up and looked out and there was Robert Love. He said, 'Have you been in the house all the time?' I said, 'Yes.' He said, 'Didn't you see the Indians?' I said, 'No.' He then told me to climb on top of the house and I would see them. I did so, and sure enough, there they were on the other side of the creek going as hard as they could go.

Love said that one of the Indians had gotten off his horse and looked into the cabin, but the door being open; not seeing anything, he though the house was empty, and there I was asleep behind the door at the time! I said, 'Hold on a minute until I get my pony, and I will go with you to town.' I had bought a pony from A.M. White the day before. I went out and found that my pony was gone! The Indians had taken him. After I found that the Indians had taken my pony, I started out to walk to Colorado City alone, Love having gone across the Monument and down that way. I had just come to the brow of the hill, going over to Colorado City, when I found our oxen and said to myself, 'They have surely got Wright this time.' I went a short distance further when I met Judge Stone, Ora Bell and one or two others. Judge Stone asked me about the boys; he was afraid they had both been killed. I told him where they were and that I thought they were *alright. He said, 'You had better go to town at once; the report has gone on ahead of you that you were killed.'*

Bell and Stone had not gone more than one hundred and fifty yards when they came to the boys, who had heard of the Indians and were headed for town. I soon heard that Charlie Everhart had been killed and that the Indians had also killed the Robbins boys and had shot Baldwin, the sheepherder. It appeared that Charlie Everhart saw the Indians coming and started for home as fast as his pony could go, but the Indians caught him near where Judge Lunt now lives, on Cascade Avenue. At the first shot he fell off his horse; the Indians ran a spear through his body and scalped him, taking every bit of hair off his head except a little fringe just above the neck.

Ben Spinney, John Hall, and I believe, Anthony Bott, and I got a team and started out to bring in the dead and wounded. We drove out from Colorado City on the main road and crossed the Monument (Creek) near the present D&RG freight depot and then went due north. We found Everhart lying there on the prairie dead, scalped and with a number of arrows sticking in his body. We returned to Colorado City and found the other dead and wounded had been brought in. David Wright, from the top of the hill on the west side of Monument Creek, saw the Indians kill Everhart, and then abandoned his ox team as too slow and ran into Colorado City and gave the alarm.

When the Cheyenne and Arapaho warriors attacked and killed Charlie Everhart and the Robbins boys in 1868, Judge E.T. Stone and sons Millard and John rode out to rescue settlers and recover their mutilated bodies which were placed on display in Doc Garvin's log cabin for all to see. Misinformation, particularly when it came to reporting Indian atrocities, was common all across the Colorado Territory. Many of the citizens of Colorado City and El Paso County refused to believe the 1868 Indian threat was real, including Mr. Robbins, the boy's father, who declined David Spielman's suggestion to herd his cattle with his so his boys wouldn't be so isolated; a decision he would regret the rest of his life. Displaying the mutilated bodies of citizens killed by warring Indians, especially the bodies of innocent women and children, would seem insensitive today. However, this was during a time when photography was new and not readily available. To encourage citizens to take this threat seriously, the bodies of these three young El Paso County victims were placed in the public for everyone to see.

There is no definitive source recording the number of people who lost their lives during the Cheyenne Wars; however, General Philip Sheridan reported to his superiors that from August through October 1868, seventy-nine civilians had been killed and nine were wounded, along with six soldiers who had been killed while another ten wounded, during skirmishes with hostile Indians. An untold number of Indians were also killed, littering the eastern plains with their skeletal remains. In El Paso County, or just north of the county line, at least fifteen residents were killed by Arapaho and Cheyenne war parties in 1868, including Job Talbert, Edward Davis, Jothan Lincoln, Jonathan Tallman, John Grief (or Griff), John Choteau, seventeen-year-old Charlie Everhart, the Robbins boys (George 11 and Franklin 8) and the youngest victim six-year-old Leona Johnson. Countless ranchers' horses and mules had been stolen during these raids, including a large herd of approximately 300 horses owned by the four Teachout brothers, stolen during a raid on September 1st on the Teachout Ranch (located just north of present-day Colorado Springs on the U.S. Air Force Academy).

Of note is an interview Scott Kelly gave to a *Gazette* newspaper reporter in 1913, Dora Foster. Her partial notes captured a few of Sheriff Kelly's words:

Twenty Plain, Cheyenne, Arapahoe and Sioux Indians...10 minutes after the Indians had scalped and killed Mrs. Tester and children on Plum Creek road, between Denver and Colorado

Springs. She kept a half-way house, Col. Shoup and 50 men were to act as guides. Outside the house they saw the soldiers coming and ran away, it was daylight near 2 o'clock.

Sheriff Kelly mentioned there were six soldiers killed, which is consistent with the total number of soldiers killed during skirmishes with Indians in 1868, and numerous horses were also stolen during these raids (some of the horses were found to have been stolen from the Teachout Ranch).

On August 10 through 14, 1868, the heaviest causalities were inflicted during the Colorado Indians Wars which raged across the eastern plains of Colorado and into the heart of El Paso County where Charlie Everhart and the Robbins boys were murdered. Although Rankin Scott Kelly had already stepped down as El Paso County Sheriff, Kelly volunteered to ride with Col. Shoup's cavalrymen to track down and kill the hostile Indians responsible, hoping of bringing an end to all the bloodshed. These many skirmishes with the hostile Indians, especially those vicious fights with the Dog Soldiers, were swift, violent, and often fought at close quarters. In one of these skirmishes, Kelly later retold how his reins were shredded and his boot was pierced by an arrow.

Author Ruth Lanza also wrote an article regarding Kelly as an Indian fighter. In this article she states the following:

He (Scott Kelly) thought the murderers were headed for Ute Pass. Kelly mounted his horse and accompanied Colonel Shoup of the United States Cavalry and about fifty soldiers in pursuit. 'We chased the Indians into a canyon', Kelly reminisced in the Colorado Springs news in 1913. 'They were in a veritable ambush, there being no outlet to the canyon. They all fought desperately. Six soldiers were killed. They lost seven horses—horses that had been stolen by the Indians from a nearby ranch. Kelly's bridle reign was cut to pieces and another arrow went through his boot. But they managed to kill the entire band of warriors.

The reference to Sheriff Kelly riding with Colonel Shoup's men, or with men who had previously fought under Colonel Shoup in the Colorado 3rd Calvary, may be technically correct; however, Shoup who had fought in the 1864 Cheyenne War at Sand Creek, had already mustered out of the U.S. military by the end of 1865 and he does not appear to be residing in the Colorado Territory in 1868. It is not known for certain where the box canyon, or the canyon without an outlet, where the fight that Kelly was involved in, or where the warriors were killed was located. However, research suggests it may have been north of El Paso County, just over the Douglas County line. Possibly as far north as the South Platte River, north of the confluence of Cherry Creek, or perhaps even further north along the Platte River, in southern Wyoming.

Another of El Paso County's early pioneers, J.B. Simms, discussed the strenuous days the settlers in Colorado City experienced in 1868 with Robert McReynolds of the *Colorado Springs Gazette* (published on September 20, 1906):

A premonition of danger warned me of danger once of lurking hostile Indians on Cottonwood Creek on the morning of December 26, 1868 resulting in a preparation for battle that probably saved my life. It was the day after Christmas; I was in the employ of the Beatty Brothers Cattle Company and was looking up some stray cattle near the head of the Cottonwood Creek, twenty miles north of Colorado City. I had been riding through the timber and was about to emerge into the open when a premonition of danger came over me. The feeling was so strong that I loosened my Henry rifle from the saddle holster and looked to the two heavy Colt revolvers I carried about me.

Half an hour passed, and while I had not yet seen anything, I could not shake off the feeling of approaching danger. Twenty minutes more and sure enough, from out of a ravine came about sixty Cheyenne and Arapaho Indians in their war paint, riding rapidly toward me. I instantly wheeled my horse and rode for a rocky butte about half a mile distance. My horse climbed the butte almost with the agility of a goat. As the bullets tore up the ground around us, I led him to behind some big rocks and then paid my respects to the advancing war party. My Henry rifle carried eighteen shots. The repeating rifle, being then unheard of by these Indians, was the greatest surprise they ever met. My first shot emptied a saddle, and then when they thought to ruse me, two or three more went down. They could not understand the rapidity of my fire, and by the time I had emptied my rifle, I had them on the run and out of range. They advanced two or three times during the day and I became amused and allowed them to come with(in) easy range, then I would turn loose as fast as I could work the rifle, and scatter them.

Author's Note - This Henry repeating rifle was likely a .44 caliber rimfire lever-action breech-loading rifle patented by Benjamin Tyler Henry in 1860 (when fully loaded it carried one round in the chamber and sixteen rounds in the loading chamber or tube). When it came to Indian fighting, the Henry rifle was a game-changer; as J.B. Simms concluded: "Late in the afternoon they gave me up as bad medicine and rode away towards Gomer's hill ("hill" may be a transcription error and could read "Gomer's Mill") where they killed a Mexican boy. From that day, I have never doubted the existence of an unseen power which may warn us of approaching danger."

One Dog Soldier, George Bent, related how Indians preferred arrows to guns for hunting and in defense since they had been trained to use the bow and arrow since they were small boys, but each arrow could be identified by its markings to the man who shot it, claiming the kill if they were raiding or hunting game.

When the Civil War broke out George Bent, known by his Cheyenne name as Ho-my-ike, had been sent away from the Colorado Territory by his famous father, William Bent, to attend an Episcopal boarding school in Kansas City, Missouri. George and several of his fellow classmates quit school and joined the Confederate Army; the Bent's after all were slaveholders. George Bent served in the Missouri State Guard and fought at the Battle of Wilson's Creek, outside of Springfield, Missouri (August 10, 1861), the First Battle of Lexington (September 20, 1861), and again at the Battle of Pea Ridge in Arkansas (March 7-8, 1862). George Bent was attached to the Missouri Cavalry, as part of General Sterling Price's division (another reported KGC member). The first two battles he fought in were decisive Confederate victories; however, the third battle was a Union victory, and afterward George was either captured or deserted, becoming a prisoner of war (POW). After swearing an oath of allegiance to the Union, George was allowed to return to his father's ranch in the Colorado Territory.

Some historians say George's younger brother, Charley Bent, known by his Cheyenne name Pe-ki-ree, which translates to White Hat in English, also fought in the Confederate Army, alongside his older brother George, during the Civil War. Charley was born in 1845, which means he would have only been 16 years of age at the Battle of Wilson's Creek; although, there were certainly younger boys fighting and dying in both armies. One of the highest-ranking Confederate cavalry officers killed in action (KIA) during the Battle of Wilson's Creek was Colonel Lewis Chivington, the older brother of Colonel John Chivington, who ordered the attack on Sand Creek. After the Massacre at Sand Creek (November 1864), both George and Charley Bent joined the Dog Soldiers and both had participated in the attack in January 1865 at Julesburg, in the northeastern Colorado Territory. The Dog Soldiers also fought in battles in the Wyoming and Nebraska Territories and western Kansas. Charley Bent was killed July 11, 1869, alongside other Dog Soldiers at the Battle of Summit Springs, Colorado Territory.

According to the research conducted by Dr. Jeff Broome for his two books, *Dog Soldier Justice* and *Cheyenne Wars (1863-1869)*, Clara Blinn and her young son, Willie, were attacked on their ranch by Cheyenne and Arapaho warriors, who were often allied with the Kiowa,

Comanche, Brule, Pawnee and even Oglala Lakota warriors. Clara and Willie Blinn tried to escape by running to a way station about seven miles east of present-day Big Timbers Museum. They were captured near where Sand Creek flows into the Arkansas River about 40 miles east of Ft. Lyons. Back east, two weeks later, on October 28, 1868, Thomas Edison (1847-1931), credited as being the inventor of the light bulb, applied for his first of 1093 patents; the electric vote recorder. But, for the early pioneers the nights out on the eastern plains of the Colorado Territory, their nights remained very dark and unimaginably scary.

On November 3, 1868, Ulysses S. Grant won the Presidential race by defeating Horatio Seymour in the U.S. Presidential election. Once Grant assumed office, his prior military leadership along with the full weight of the federal government would be brought to bear to drive an end to the Indian Wars in the West.

With the signing of the Medicine Lodge Treaty, the Southern Cheyenne and Arapaho were now forced to leave their traditional territory, in Colorado and Kansas, to settle onto another existing reservation in Indian County (near present-day Cheyenne, Oklahoma); however, not all of the Cheyenne Chiefs signed the treaty and some of the raids continued.

On November 27, 1868, the Battle of Washita River was fought when Lt. Col. George Armstrong Custer's 7th Cavalry attacked an unsuspecting Cheyenne encampment with about 50 lodges under Chief Black Kettle. Clara Blinn and her son Willie were killed during Custer's attack to prevent them from being rescued. Their bodies were not discovered until Generals Sheridan and Custer revisited the Washita about two weeks after Custer's fight. Further downriver, near an oxbow bend, was a second encampment of about 129 lodges established under the Arapaho Chief Little Raven. The night before the attack, a war party consisting of approximately 150, including Dog Soldiers, had raided a white settlement along the Smoky Hill River. Following the war party's tracks, Osage scouts for the 7th Cavalry followed their tracks in the snow to the villages on the Washita River.

Similar to the controversy of whether Sand Creek was a Massacre or a Battle, Custer's surprise attack on the Cheyenne and Arapaho villages would also be embroiled in controversy. Case in point; according to an article later printed in the *New York Tribute,* dated December 14, 1868:

Col. Wynkoop, agent for the Cheyenne and Arapahoe Indians, has published his letter of resignation. He regards Gen. Custer's late fight as simply a massacre, and says that Black Kettle and his band, friendly Indians, were, when attacked, on their way to their reservation.

The problems at Black Kettle's encampment on the Washita River in 1868, as well as at Sand Creek in 1864, at least some of those allowed to join the Chief's camp were Dog Soldiers. Black Kettle and his wife, survivors of the Sand Creek Massacre, were among the 103 Cheyenne and Arapaho killed. The 7th Cavalry lost 21 men listed as killed and another 13 wounded. The U.S. military could replenish their losses, but the Dog Soldiers could not.

George Shoup was later appointed Governor of Idaho Territory in 1888 and was elected to the U.S. Senate (1890) when Idaho became a State (a statute of George L. Shoup stands today in Statuary Hall, of the U.S. Capitol Building, Washington, D.C.). Shoup Road in the Black Forest of eastern El Paso County is not named for the former Governor of Idaho; however, it is named honoring a former Governor of Colorado, Oliver Henry Shoup, who served as the 22nd Governor of Colorado (1919-1923). Oliver Henry Shoup had been born in Champaign County, Illinois, and when he was 13 he moved with his parents to Colorado Springs, Colorado. Oliver Shoup owned a successful cattle ranch in eastern El Paso County and died of a heart attack in his home in Colorado Springs in 1940.

Scott Kelly – Land Owner

While serving as Sheriff, Scott Kelly owned a ranch along Fountain Creek. Changes and events that were happening around the country after the end of the Civil War motivated Kelly to give up his dream of working his ranch along Fountain Creek. Kelly would focus on fighting in the Indian Wars. Rankin Scott Kelly sold his ranch along the creek to Dora Foster's parents, Marcus and Lizzie Foster in 1867. Dora Foster was the *Gazette* reporter that would interview and write about Rankin in his later life.

Kelly had been part of the Foster's family life for a long time. In one article by Dora Foster, titled "Pikes Peak Region Yesterdays", she wrote the following:

In the autumn of 1862 my mother tells that one Sunday afternoon she drove with Scott (Kelly) through what is now Ivywild, and passed through fields of wheat which were growing beside the narrow roadway, and that Scott reached out with his long whip touching the wheat as they passed. Two beautiful sorrel ponies took them swiftly along till they reached the crossing of Cheyenne Creek, which is now near the end of Wolf Ave and Cheyenne Rd.

They saw a young man crossing deftly from one stone to another across the rushing water. Before the flood of 1864 Cheyenne Creek came down what is now the north side of Cheyenne Rd, and because there was no water taken out in pipe as there is now, there was plenty of water to be crossed. Mother admired the young man's graceful jumping from one stone to another and asked Scott who he might be, "He is a young carpenter from the East who is staying at a hotel in Colorado City, his name is Foster." That was the first glimpse my mother had of my father.

As the Cheyenne Wars trickled to an end, driven in part by the deaths of so many of the Dog Soldiers and most of their known War Chiefs, Scott Kelly returned to ranching in El Paso County where he had purchased two adjoining eighty-acre tracks of land from Augustine Peralta on June 1, 1868. The official deed of transfer for 160 acres of land from Augustine Peralta to Rankin S. Kelly reads in part as follows; "as assignee, as aforesaid, and to his heirs," has been located establishing, "Augustine Peralta Packer Captain Gonzales Company New Mexico Volunteers Navajo Indian War" was granted a deed to 160 acres in recognition of his military service during the Civil War. Augustine Peralta had served a Packer or teamster with the New Mexico Volunteers, where soldiers from the Colorado 1st Regiment Volunteer had fought and died at Peralta in 1861. A soldier from the Colorado First Regiment, Ovando Hollister, who fought against the Rebels at Peralta, seemed rather unimpressed by the contributions of the New Mexico Volunteers, at least during the Battle at the town of Peralta.

This Land Patent, transferring ownership of the ranch from Augustine Peralta to Rankin S. Kelly, is land that today is occupied by the Shriner's Mule Barn east of I-25 and north of South Academy Blvd, in Colorado Springs, Colorado. The east property line for the 160 acres extends east across Fountain Creek and coincidentally abuts up against the western edge of the current El Paso County Jail. The land title "granting Bounty Land to certain Officers and Soldiers who have been engaged in the military service of the United States" was signed by U.S. President Andrew Johnson, on June 1, 1868. Six months later, on Christmas Day, December 25, 1868, President Andrew Johnson signed another document that granted an unconditional pardon to all Civil War rebels. CSA President Jefferson Davis was specifically excluded; however, all CSA Generals, including Henry Hopkins Sibley, Ben McCulloch, Nathan Bedford Forrest, Albert Pike, and Cherokee Chiefs Stand Watie and John Ross, and other suspected KGC members, including outlaws James D. Clarke and Jesse James, received U.S. Presidential pardons.

As Kelly was settling down to life on the ranch, a new town was about to be born in El Paso County, Colorado Springs, with its founder William Jackson Palmer. On February 5, 1869, prospectors in Victoria, Australia, had discovered the largest alluvial gold nugget in history; it was named the "Welcome Stranger." A welcomed stranger to Colorado City in 1869 was 32-year-old General William Jackson Palmer, who stepped down from a stagecoach for breakfast while it stopped for a team of fresh horses. This one-stage stop would forever change General Palmer and General Palmer would forever change El Paso County. After the Civil War, General Palmer had been employed as the secretary and treasurer of the Kansas Pacific Railway responsible for extending service through south-central Colorado. General Palmer envisioned a north-to-south railroad connecting Denver City to Mexico City; following the Front Range of the Rocky Mountains and extending southward along the Rio Grande River.

On July 26, 1869, General William Jackson Palmer, while working as the chief engineer for the Kansas Pacific railroad, traveled through El Paso County and wrote his fiancé Mary Lincoln Mellen, sharing his feelings about the Pikes Peak Region:

The night ride was by moonlight. I spread out my blanket on top of the coach—back of a very sociable and obliging driver—and slept soundly in the fresh air, until wakened by the round moon looking steadily into my face when I found the magnificent Pikes Peak towering immediately about at an elevation of over 14,000 ft., topped with a little snow. I could not sleep any more with all the splendid panorama of mountains gradually unrolling itself, as the moon faded and the sun began to rise, but sleepy though I was, I sat up and drank in, along with the purest mountain air, the full exhilaration of the morning ride." "At Colorado city—'the Garden of the Gods'—we stopped to take breakfast. I freshened up by a preliminary bath in the waters of the 'Fountain' whose valley we had followed all night and morning. Near here are the finest springs of soda—and the most enticing scenery. I am sure there will be a famous resort here soon after the railroad reaches Denver. If I go back the same way I shall try to stop at the 'Garden of the Gods' and run up to the summit of Ute Pass to take a look over into the South Park...I somehow fancied that an exploration of the dancing little tributaries of 'Monument' or 'Fountain' might disclose somewhere up near to where they come leaping with delight from the cavernous wall of the Rocky Mountains, perhaps some charming spot which might be made a future home.

Palmer hired Irving Howbert, son of Reverend Howbert, to assist him in acquiring the land he would need to establish the Fountain Town Colony (later renamed the Colorado Springs Town Company) along Monument Creek, north of the confluence of Fountain Creek. Rather than building his Denver and Rio Grande Railroad to Colorado City, and paying higher prices for the land to support his railroad depot, Palmer decided his railroad would follow Monument Creek, which empties into Fountain Creek, then flows south through El Paso County to Pueblo County. Palmer used the same business strategy in Pueblo County; rather than extending his railroad to a town, he would lay his tracks just outside of the existing city's limits and let the town come to him.

General Palmer had also realized the geographical value offered in the valley at the confluence of Monument and Fountain Creeks, near where Governor Juan Bautista de Anza had attacked Cuero Verde's main camp. This was also in the same valley where Charlie Everhart, the Robbins boys, and the sheepherder Judge Baldwin, were attacked by the Cheyenne warriors. Palmer knew this site would make a perfect stop for the Denver & Rio Grande railroad he intended to build connecting Denver to Santa Fe and beyond. By the winter of 1869 Palmer had decided to build a resort on that site and began buying land, including a purchase of land that totaled nearly 10,000 acres, from the U.S. government for about $1 an acre.

In his book, *Memories of a Lifetime in the Pike's Peak Region*, Irving Howbert writes about the time and the area when General Palmer first arrived in the Pikes Peak Region:

Up to the time of the founding of Colorado Springs, there were large herds of wild horses in the eastern part of El Paso County and adjacent country...General Palmer, the founder of Colorado Springs, in a letter written in September, 1869, says that on a trip taken that year from Fort Sheridan, terminus of the Kansas Pacific Railway, directly across the country to the present town site of Colorado Springs, he saw many buffalo, three herds of wild horses, and antelope in such numbers that he was seldom out of sight of them.

The land Palmer accumulated to establish the Fountain Town, extended east from Limit Street, the eastern edge of Colorado City, across Monument Creek to the east, then north and south following Monument Creek. In June 1871 General Palmer drove the first stake in the ground at the southeast corner of today's Pikes Peak Avenue and Cascade Avenue, to establish Colorado Springs, Colorado. General Palmer used the surveying skills of another Civil War General, Robert A. Cameron, to plat Colorado Springs, directing Cameron, "Take your center line from here to the summit, reverse your instrument, and you have Pikes Peak Avenue." All the east/west streets ran parallel to Pikes Peak Avenue and all the north/south streets were laid out at 90-degree angles. If one stands at that location today and looks to the summit of Pikes Peak, they will see what is today known as "Cameron Cone" at the elevation of 10,707 ft., a fully forested prominence just to the left of the view. Named as such to honor General Robert A. Cameron, the man that platted out the city below.

On March 4, 1969, another Civil War General, Ulysses S. Grant, was elected to serve as the 18th President of the United States, succeeding President Andrew Johnson, who had stepped in after the assassination of President Abraham Lincoln. In El Paso County, Sheriff Aaron Mason, who had succeeded Sheriff Kelly, continued to serve as Sheriff until stepping down three years later. On May 10, 1869, the First Transcontinental Railroad in North America was finally completed at Promontory, Utah. This significant historic event in American history was celebrated by driving a commemorative last spike made of gold at the intersection of these two great railroads. With railroad tracks laid in place that now surrounded the Southern Cheyenne and Arapaho tribes, the military could rapidly transport fresh troops, horses, and military equipment almost anywhere in the West. It would be the Iron Horse that would soon drive the last stake into the chest of the last free Plains Indians in the American West.

California and Back

Rankin Scott Kelly left El Paso County after selling his land to General William Palmer sometime in the early 1870s. From a later interview, we discover Kelly made it to the Pacific Ocean, where he purchased another ranch in California. However, according to an interview he later gave to Dora Foster: "He learned a short time later that his property was near the headquarters of a band of horse thieves and road agents, and soon left that part of the country."

Being a sheriff in the Colorado Territory, during the Civil War, a low profile could still be maintained due to poor communications with the east. Kelly still had in the back of his mind that he was still wanted in Maine for murder. The last thing Kelly wanted was to be anywhere near where he could be associated with criminals. Kelly was still avoiding Census reports and was not found in the 1870 census. The census does show that his older brother and a sister or possibly a sister-in-law, and their family were still in Houlton, Maine. Kelly's family would not have known of his military service during the Mexican-American War or his courageous service as the first Sheriff of El Paso County. Kelly would never know his nieces or nephew.

On August 1, 1876, President Ulysses S. Grant signed the

proclamation declaring Colorado the 38th State of the United States. Colorado was named the Centennial State, being established one hundred years after the signing of the Declaration of Independence in 1776.

We learn Kelly returned to Colorado in the late 1870s. In 1877 there is an advertisement in the local Leadville papers for the Kelly Stables. *The Leadville Gazetteer* also lists "Kelly, R. S. bds. (boards) 227 W. 2nd St South" (the original house has been replaced, although an old barn off the alley appears period to the late 19th Century). After leaving California, Rankin Scott Kelly arrived in the right place at the right time to participate in Colorado's Silver Boom. Although silver had been discovered during the Colorado Gold Rush in 1859, in Clear Creek County, mining silver wasn't profitable until the U.S. Congress authorized the free coinage of silver in 1878. By the spring of 1879, the gullies around Leadville and the surrounding mountains were swarming with miners with dreams of striking it rich. Kelly was there when over $82 million in silver would be mined in Colorado, just twenty years after the Colorado Gold Rush.

Mining records show that along with a handful of other miners, Kelly invested $10,000 in a silver mine. The mining claim was protested and a civil action was eventually settled with Kelly paying $1.00 for the settlement of the lawsuit. Kelly then claimed another mine in the "Diamond Group MS 14432" northwest of Leadville, near Mosquito Pass (elevation 13,188 feet) which he names the Rankin mine. Although Kelly may not have struck it rich in Leadville; however, another of Colorado City's early pioneers did and became known as Colorado's Silver King. Horace Tabor and his wife Augusta had owned one of the first houses built in Colorado City in 1860 and certainly would have known Sheriff Kelly. Tabor's famous Matchless Mine can still be found northwest of Leadville, Colorado, not far from a far less famous mine, the Rankin.

In 1880 U.S. Census for Leadville showed a population of 23,000; of which 18,000 were males and 5,000 women, only half of whom were reportedly "respectable". The other half were ladies with names like "Red Stockings," who were counted among Leadville's soiled doves, ladies of the evening, fallen women, and members of the frail sisterhood. When Lady Red Stockings finally moved away from Leadville, she took with her over $100,000 in cash, money she earned from mining the miners.

Colorado City, the center of El Paso County, also had prostitution, but it was not a problem in the early times when Kelly was Sheriff, as the town was too small. A red-light district would give future sheriffs problems in the late 1800s when more men moved to the area and several brothels were built. Laura Bell, for example, was a very popular "Queen of the Tenderloin" and was listed in the 1888 Colorado City business directory. Madam Bell was known to have had various suitors, including the ever-dashing John "Prairie Dog" O'Byrne. Up until 1890, Prairie Dog would pull up in front of Laura Bell's, always somewhat inebriated, to pick Laura Bell in his buggy, pulled by two huge elk, named "Thunder and Button." One slight disadvantage with Thunder and Button, as opposed to more traditional animals, such as a team of horses taught to pull a buggy, was these two fully grown elk, each adorned with a massive antler rack, had but one speed; full out at 30 mph! Thunder and Button would charge ahead, scaring horses and infuriating all the respectable women of Colorado Springs; Colorado City's gentler yet less tolerant sister city by the close of the nineteenth century.

From Leadville, the ever-mobile Kelly moved on to Ouray, Colorado. As he grew older Kelly it seems was worried less about his past and even appears in the twelfth U.S. Census. The Census for Precinct 12 Ouray, Colorado dated the 14th day of June 1900 records the following entry:

NAME: Kelly, Rankin S., RELATIONSHIP (of each person to head of household): Boarder, COLOR of Race/Sex: White Male, DATE of Birth (Month/Year): July 1828, AGE at last birthday: 71, MARTIAL Status: Single, PLACE of Birth: Canada (Eng.), BIRTH Place of Father: Ireland, BIRTH Place of Mother: Canadian (English), CITIZENSHIP Year of Immigration to the United States: 1861, Number of Years in United States: 39,

Naturalization: Yes (Naturalized): OCCUPATION: Teamster, EDUCATION (Can read, can write, can understand English): Yes, Yes, Yes.

This U.S. Census does reveal several interesting personal facts about Rankin S. Kelly. He became a naturalized U.S. Citizen in 1861, the year Colorado became a U.S. Territory, and the year Kelly was appointed to serve as the first El Paso County Sheriff. However, there are still several gaps in his life's story that remain mysterious. For example, if it is accurate that he had been in the U.S. for 39 years, at age 71, where was Rankin Scott Kelly during the missing 32 years? Perhaps these were the years he felt were best left forgotten. Did he return to where his father was born in Ireland or remain somewhere in Canada where he and his mother had been born? Since we know he was born in 1828 and ran away from home at age 14 (1842) where did he spend the four years between 1842-1846, before he enlisted in the U.S. military to fight in the Mexican-American War? These are the questions Kelly likely did not want to answer.

On March 26, 1901, the *Ouray Herald* reported Rankin Kelly was one of seven men dismissed from the hospital, and on September 23, 1901:

The following (16) bills were presented and allowed on the Poor Fund (including) Sisters of Mercy Care Rankin Kelly $85.60.

The original St. Joseph's Miner's Hospital in Ouray, Colorado, where Kelly was hospitalized for several months, was built in 1886 for the miners of the adjoining San Juan Mountain region of Colorado. The hospital was initially operated by the Sisters of Mercy, all of whom came from either Durango, Colorado, or Omaha, Nebraska. The hospital remained operational until 1964 when the Ouray County Historical Society (OCHS) Museum began exhibiting in the building which they bought in 1976. The building consists of three floors and

38 exhibit rooms, which remains much the same as when Scott Kelly was a patient.

On March 13, 1909, William Jackson Palmer passed away in his home Glen Eyrie. His legacy includes many financial donations and endowments in Colorado Springs including those he made to Colorado College founded in 1874, Colorado School for the Deaf and Blind also founded in 1874, and a tuberculosis sanitarium which was later re-founded in 1965 as the University of Colorado at Colorado Springs. He had also made a significant contribution to a traditionally all-black college immediately following the Civil War, today's Hampton University, founded in 1868 to provide education for "freedmen", near Fort Monroe (the Freedom Fort) at Hampton, Virginia. Today there are two Palmer Halls that stand named in honor and gratitude of General William Jackson Palmer; one a Colorado College in Colorado Springs, the other Hampton University, in Hampton, Virginia. Also, today for the public to enjoy is Glen Eryie, Palmer's home on the land he bought from Kelly.

Late in life, Kelly was suffering from health problems and still living in Ouray at the turn of the 20th century. In searching the local newspaper achieves for Ouray County during that time frame, we find mentions of Scott Kelly in the *Ouray Herald* for Christmas December 25, 1908: "Rankin Kelly is slightly improved from heart trouble and cancer of the stomach." Again, New Year's Day, January 1, 1909: "Rankin Kelly, who is 83 years of age and suffering from cancer of the stomach, is not doing very well." Then again on March 12, 1910: "Rankin Kelly is up and around and is feeling sad because of today being the 80th anniversary of his mother's being drowned." The 1910 Census still lists him as a resident of Ouray, Colorado.

Sheriff Kelly Returns After 40 Years

Rankin Scott Kelly returned to visit Colorado City for the first time in 1913. At the age of 87, it had been over forty years since Sheriff Kelly had stepped foot in El Paso County. Kelly returned just a few months before his death. He had been previously hospitalized for heart troubles and must have known he was slowly dying of stomach cancer. The lower altitude may have been encouraged by his doctors at the Sisters of Mercy hospital in Ouray. An article in the *Colorado Springs Gazette Telegraph* on May 23, 1913, tells of his return:

First El Paso County Sheriff Visiting Here: Scott Kelly, one of the region's early pioneers and a member of the colony that settled in Colorado City, is visiting friends here for the first time in almost 40 years. He is the guest of Anthony Bott, one of the founders of Colorado City. Kelly was the first sheriff of El Paso County, and was a terror to all law breakers within his jurisdiction. In the early days he sold what later became known as the Glen Eyrie property to General William J. Palmer for $1,000, investing the money in a ranch in the San Joaquin Valley, California. He learned a short time later that his property was near the headquarters of a band *of horse thieves and road agents, and soon left that part of the country. During the last quarter of a century Kelly has made his home in Ouray, Colo. He expects to spend several days in Colorado City and the Pikes Peak region looking up old friends.*

Perhaps Kelly returned to where he may have felt most at home, a place he helped to build, Colorado City. By 1913 Colorado Springs had become known across the country as a place known for its world-class health care; where Kelly felt he could rest and recover from his health issues. No doubt much had changed in the forty years Rankin Scott Kelly had been away from El Paso County. When he left, General William Jackson Palmer had just founded the Colorado Springs Company, driving the first stake in the ground at the southeast corner of Pikes Peak Avenue and Cascade Avenue in 1871. The town was laid out with the north-south streets named after mountain ranges and the east-west streets after rivers across the U.S. (going south to north, east to west). The main streets were at least 100 feet wide, allowing enough room that a man could turn a freight drawn wagon around in the street without having to back it up.

Rankin's friend and fellow early pioneer M.S. Beach had become involved in several mining endeavors, including mining for silver in the San Juan Mountains. Colorado City's growth had slowed considerably since Beach had first helped build the cabin Dr. Garvin had once used for his home and office. The log cabin went from being the first Colorado Territorial Legislative Building to the El Paso County Administration Building, to becoming Sam Wah's Laundry. Kelly may have been surprised to learn that on September 9th, 1873, the voters of El Paso County had voted to move the county seat from Colorado City to Colorado Springs. He would have been impressed by the red brick Colorado Territory Jail that had been built in 1875 in downtown Colorado Spring, which would serve as El Paso County's jail for more than a century.

In 1903 the 9th and largest El Paso County Courthouse was built in "Alamo Park" which is home to today's Colorado Springs Pioneer's Museum (the building had been used for 58 years as a courthouse until 1961). The building had been built with funds donated by multi-millionaire William Scott Stratton and when it was first occupied it contain offices for all elected El Paso County officials, including the Sheriff's Office which was originally located on the top floor in the southeast corner. As the Sheriff's Office expanded they ran out of room and were relocated to the west end of the basement where they remained until 1976. Then a new Sheriff's office was built across Tejon Street to the west. When the new Sheriff's Office was built it had a more modern jail and the old Colorado Territorial Jail across the street on the west side of Cascade Avenue was torn down to make room for other county administrative buildings, including today's Centennial Hall and Pikes Peak Center.

Not only had El Paso County and Colorado Springs witnessed dramatic change since Kelly had been away, but the world itself had undergone a dramatic transformation. In 1882 Thomas Edison founded the Edison Illumination Company providing electricity for 59 customers lighting the first homes in New York City. At the same time, the first light switch was thrown in any American city, General Palmer also turned on electric lights to illuminate his castle in Glen Eyrie. On July 22, 1893, Katheryn Lee Bates, a visiting college professor from Wellesley College, had taken a break from her summer teaching duties at Colorado College, to go to the summit of Pikes Peak. Throughout her summer travels, Katheryn Lee Bates had been working on the words to a poem capturing the beauty she had seen along her trip. After returning to her room at the Antler's Hotel, she wrote about the "Purple mountain's majesty above the fruited plains," in her poem which she initially titled "Pike's Peak", later changing it to "America the Beautiful" which was afterward put to music and known today as one of American's most patriotic songs.

One of the amazing developments Rankin Scott Kelly certainly would have enjoyed would have been the beautiful new library, constructed in 1904, two blocks from where he was staying with his friend Anthony Bott in Old Colorado City. The library at 2418 W. Pikes Peak Ave was built using funds provided by the Carnegie Corporation of New York. Two more Carnegie-funded libraries had also been built in El Paso County—one constructed in downtown Colorado Springs in 1905 and another in Manitou Springs in 1911. In total there were hundreds of Carnegie Libraries constructed across the country from 1899 to 1917. Each library was built by the local community that applied for a grant for the construction of the building and books. Andrew Carnegie, a Scottish immigrant, the son of poor parents, had become one of the richest men in America. At the time of his death, August 11, 1919, Andrew Carnegie had given away $350, 695, 653 (approximately $4.75 billion in today's dollars), becoming a leader of philanthropy across the United States and the British Empire.

Kelly would have enjoyed sitting in the Carnegie Library reading stories about how Wilbur and Orville Wright had flown their first air airplane in Kitty Hawk, North Carolina, in 1903 and then taught the rest of the world how to fly. Headlines reported that on October 10, 1913, President Woodrow Wilson had triggered the explosion of the Gamboa Dike, which officially ended construction on the Panama Canal, linking the Atlantic Ocean to the Pacific Ocean. Cars were becoming commonplace on the streets of Colorado Springs. General Palmer had purchased the first two automobiles in El Paso County just a few years prior to his death in 1909. On December 1, 1913, the Ford Motor Company introduced the first moving assembly line, reducing chassis assembly time from 12½ hours to 2 hours, 40 minutes.

Headlines in the local newspaper read—on March 13, 1913, Mexican Revolution leader Poncho Villa returned to Mexico from a self-imposed exile to the U.S.; on April 24, 1913, the Woolworth Building opened in New York City and was designated the tallest building in the world at 57 stories, built at a cost of $13.5 million dollars. The last Shan Kiev of the Ute Nation was held in the summer of 1913 at the beautiful Garden of the Gods north of Colorado City. Fifty-six people, including fifty-two

Ute, gathered to have their photo taken in front of the standing red rock; pictured in the middle was a Ute woman sitting on the ground identified, "The widow of Chief Ouray, venerable Chipeta."

When Scott Kelly returned to El Paso County, he found that in addition to Andrew Carnegie, the citizens were fortunate to have had other generous benefactors as well, among the first was Winfield Scott Stratton. Stratton, a carpenter like Scott Kelly, had first come to Colorado City in 1868 to mine for gold and silver in Colorado's Mountains, working as a carpenter during the winter months. On July 4, 1891, Stratton awoke from a dream, where he claimed he had a vision, showing him where he would find gold. Stratton struck it rich, naming the mine the Independence Mine since he discovered it on Independence Day. Many other miners followed Stratton's lead and the Cripple Creek area exploded. The population of Cripple Creek soon surpassed that of Colorado City and Colorado Springs combined. A vote was taken to establish a separate county and Teller County was carved out of the western portion of El Paso County in 1899; however, the majestic Pikes Peak remained part of El Paso County.

Winfield Scott Stratton almost certainly would have known Scott Kelly, and of course, most everyone would have known Sheriff Kelly. Stratton extracted $11 million in gold from the Independence Mine and then sold his mine to a London investment company for another $10 million. When Stratton died on September 14, 1902, he left most of his wealth to establish the Myron Stratton Home, for aged poor, and dependent children, which he named after his father. The Myron Stratton Home opened on Thanksgiving Day, November 27, 1913, and Rankin Scott Kelly was admitted as its first resident. At age 87, with no pension or family, Kelly certainly qualified as "aged poor" but was too proud to accept charity; so Kelly's friends, Anthony Bott and Irving Howbert arranged for him to live at the home and work as the night watchman.

On November 27, 1913, the *Colorado Springs Evening Telegraph* ran this story:

Scott Kelley, First Sheriff of County, Watchman at Home. Scott Kelley, the first sheriff of El Paso county and one of the three oldest pioneers of the Pikes Peak region, has been appointed watchman at the Myron Stratton home and will begin his duties at once. The home will be open for the adults who are to occupy the cottages next week and Superintendent Cowan is this week getting his home furnished and moving his office fixtures. Mr. Kelly was one of the remarkable figures at the Pioneer ball last night and in spite of his 87 years danced as lively as a college boy. He has had a remarkable record as a peace officer and will make an admirable watchman as he has a fine record for faithfulness to duty.

On December 5, 1913, a record-breaking snowstorm struck the Colorado Springs area depositing up to five feet of snow in some places. The devastating blizzard closed all the schools and most businesses, as the roads became completely impassable. In Colorado Springs and elsewhere across El Paso County, the fridged temperatures froze water pipes, including those underground at the Myron Stratton Home. Despite his age and frail health, the Home's faithful night watchman, Rankin Scott Kelly, put on both his suits of clothes, then donned several pairs of socks, before setting out to make his nightly rounds. From being out in the cold that night Rankin Scott Kelly caught pneumonia and died a few days later at the age of 87 at the Myron Stratton Home on December 30, 1913.

Shortly before his death, Scott Kelly was interviewed by Dora Ines Foster, the family friend and newspaper reporter for the *Colorado Springs Gazette Telegraph*. Dora Foster's parents, Mr. and Mrs. Marcus A. Foster, had been personal friends of Scott Kelly in the early 1860s and purchased his ranch in 1867 which had been located on Fountain Creek just south of Colorado Springs. Dora Foster published her interview with Sheriff Kelly in her book *Colorado Yesterdays*, which tells several of her experiences growing up in the Pikes Peak region. One chapter she devotes to "The First Sheriff of El Paso County" offers readers a glimpse of what Kelly experienced when, he came to Colorado on June 5th, 1860. Dora Foster said of Rankin:

He was a mystery insofar as his early life was known—refusing to speak of his past before he came to Colorado. When asked about it, he would reply, 'I have my reasons for not telling.' And not until near the end of his life of 87 years did his friends know of his boyhood, nor of his birthplace. He refused to tell even the young woman he wished to marry.

Although there might be a few young men in that early day in Colorado City (1860) whose past histories would not bear looking into, Scott Kelly was not among them since his honesty, frankness and sincere desire to do right soon won for him the respect and admiration of all, and his fearlessness was so well recognized that he was elected to the office of county sheriff. He often said during the four years he held the office, 'Indian fighting was my business.'

Scott Kelly never married, telling that the only girl he had ever wished to marry had married someone else, a fact that my mother and father knew well. Twenty-four years in his later life he made his home in a little cabin on a hillside in Ouray, Colo., where he had for company a cat and a cow, as well as many friends, among whom he counted the late Irving Howbert of Colorado Springs.

A few months before the opening of the Myron Stratton Home, Kelly returned from Ouray for a short visit and to ask Irving Howbert for his aid in securing for him a job in the Home, as he refused to enter on any other conditions. So thru Mr. Howbert's help he was given the position as engineer for the Home, and in the autumn of 1913 he came back to undertake that work. That same summer while Kelly was visiting in our home he went one afternoon to sit in the South, or Alamo, Park, to wait for a Canon streetcar, and there fell into a conversation with a man and his wife who were visiting here from Houlton, Maine.

Fearfully and cautiously Kelly had asked them concerning some of his old friends there in that town and finally they spoke the name of the young man whom Kelly had though he had killed so long ago. Then to Kelly's wondrous joy and relief they told him the Emitt, tho an old man, was still living there in the town tho retired from business was in good health.

It was an excited old man who rushed home to tell mother and father of his happy discovery, that the man he had supposed he had killed was still living.

While acting as engineer in the Myron Stratton Home that autumn an early freeze occurred and poor Mr. Kelly, then nearly 87, woke one morning to find many of the water pipes frozen and since he told that someone spoke sharply to him about his neglect, he dressed himself with both his suits of clothes, put on several pairs of socks and taking a cane struck out to walk to my parent's home thru about two feet of snow. A truck driver came upon him leaning against a snow bank, almost exhausted, and brought him to us. He remained in our home for a week or so, when my father persuaded him to return to the Home as an inmate. Realizing that his life was nearing its end he asked no help but said: 'Spend no money on me. Give me only a pine box and lay me away in that. I am used to pine boxes.' But after his death the El Paso County Pioneers Association, with the kindly help of David F. Law, gave him a royal funeral service and a handsome coffin. The associate purchased a lot in Evergreen Cemetery, marking his last resting place with a simple stone.

The *Colorado Springs Evening Telegraph*, Tuesday, December 30, 1913, carried this headline, "R.S. Kelley, First Sheriff of El Paso County, Dies." The subheading read, "One of the Most Picturesque Characters in Colorado History Passes Away— First Person Admitted to Stratton Home." The article states the following:

Rankin Scott Kelly, aged 87 years, El Paso County's first sheriff, the terror of desperadoes who roamed the Rockies in the early '60s, died at the Myron Stratton home at 4:30 o'clock this morning. The man who had laughed at death hundreds of times when he matched nerve and wits and unerring aim with the most desperate criminals known in the west, died from enlargement of the heart resulting from nephritis. Although he had been ailing for several days his death was unexpected.

Kelly was the first person admitted to the Stratton home, going there on Thanksgiving Day. Too proud to accept charity, he declined to enter the home unless given work there so that he might earn wages. He was nominally a watchman and fireman. On December 5, the day after the big snow storm, he became angry because the nurse at the home wished him to take some medicine and walked to the home of M.A. Foster, an old pioneer on Cheyenne boulevard, near the Zoo. He was cared for there for several days and then taken back to the home where he was given every care. Last night he ate a hearty meal and said he was feeling fine. At 4:30 o'clock this morning death suddenly claimed him.

In many respects Kelly was one of the most picturesque figures in early Colorado history. He was one of the most virile men the west has known. He was a man of indomitable courage and his greatest boast was that he never "hit the back trail" for anyone or anything. Kelly attended practically all of the practice dances before the Pioneer ball given by the El Paso County Pioneer association, Thanksgiving eve, in Temple Theater. But owning to a slight illness, he was unable to be present at the ball. This was one of the most bitter disappointments he had experienced in years.

Whether Kelly has any living relatives is not known. Several years ago he had a brother in business in Cincinnati, O., and a sister, Miss Katherine Kelley, living in Chatham, New Brunswick, Canada. He had not heard from them for a long time. Kelly never married. He said he was always too busy. For several years he lived in Leadville and Ouray, returning to Colorado Springs the last time a little less than a year ago. Funeral arrangements have not been made.

The funeral will be held tomorrow afternoon at 2:30 o'clock from the D. F. Law undertaking rooms, the Rev. J. H. Spencer officiating.

The modest tombstone marking Lot 84 in Block 57 at Evergreen Cemetery in Colorado Springs reads, "R. Scott Kelly First Sheriff of El Paso CO Died Dec. 30 1913, Aged 87 Yrs." The large granite tombstone next to Scott Kelly's is engraved, "Melancthon Sayre Beach Joined the Pioneers October 19, 1917." As twilight falls late each spring the shadows of these two gravestones merge with many other El Paso County's early pioneers to join the long shadow cast from Pikes Peak. During the last interview with newspaper reporter Dora Foster shortly before he died, Dora asked what it was like to know the man he thought he had killed was still alive. Sheriff Kelly replied, "I'm glad to know that before I go over yonder, my hands are clean."

1.   Rankin Scott Kelly 1861–1867
2.   Bert Myers 1866 (3 Days)
3.   Aaron Mason 1867–1871
4.   Robert Donelly 1871–1873
5.   Cornelius Eubank 1873–1876
6.   Peter Becker 1876–1879
7.   W.A. Smith 1880–1882
8.   Loren C. Dana 1883–1887
9.   Leonard Jackson 1887–1892
10.   M.E. Bowers 1892–1896
11.   Winfield S. Boynton 1896–1899
12.   Donald C. Gaddard 1900–1901
13.   William R. Gilbert 1902–1904
14.   Oliver P. Grimes 1905–1908
15.   C.G. Birdsall 1909–1917
16.   J.H. Weir 1917–1922
17.   S.R. Berkley 1923–1926
18.   R.M. Jackson 1927–1934
19.   Samuel Deal 1935–1946
20.   Ray Slocum 1946–1948
21.   Norman E. Short 1949–1954
22.   Earl Sullivan 1955–1975
23.   Marion Shipley 1975–1979
24.   Harold (Red) Davis 1979–1983
25.   Bernard Barry 1983–1995
26.   John Anderson 1995–2003
27.   Terry Meketa 2003–2014
28.   Bill Elder 2014 –

References and Recommended Reading

Anderson, John Wesley. *Ute Indian Prayer Trees of the Pikes Peak Region*, Circle Star Publishing, Colorado Springs, Colorado, 2015

Barbaro, Barbara J. Law and Disorder in Colorado City 1859-1917, Old Colorado City Historical Society, Colorado Springs, Co., 2009

Broome, Jeff. Cheyenne War, Indian Raids on the Roads to Denver 1864-1869, Aberdeen Books, Sheridan, Colorado, 2013
- - - . *Dog Soldier Justice, The Ordeal of Susanna Alderdice in the Kansas Indian War*, University of Nebraska Press, Lincoln, Nebraska, 2003

Campbell, Jeff C., *Sand Creek Massacre, Background Booklet #1 & #2, 1st Regiment Cavalry, Colorado Volunteers, United States Army Volunteers*, Kiowa County Press, Plains Printing, Inc., Eads, Colorado 81036, 2002-2006

Carson, Phil. *Across the Northern Frontier, Spanish Explorations in Colorado.* Johnson Books, Boulder, Colorado, 1998
- - -. *Essays and Monographs in Colorado History*, Essays Number 14 1994, The Colorado Historical Society, Denver, Colorado, 1995
- - -. Fort Garland Museum, A Capsule History and Guide, A Museum of The Colorado Historical Society, Denver, Colorado, 2005

Claypool, Mary C. and Oldach, Denise R.W., *Here Lies Colorado Springs: Historical Figures buried in Evergreen and Fairview Cemeteries*, City of Colorado Springs, 1995

Compton, Ralph. *The Santa Fe Trail*, St. Martin's Paperbacks, 1997

Davant, Jeanne. *Wellsprings, A History of the Pikes Peak Region*, Gazette Enterprises, Colorado Springs, Colorado, 2001

Decker, Peter R. *The Utes Must Go! American Expansion and the Removal of a People*, Fulcrum Publishing, Golden, Colorado, 2004

Ellis, Amanda M. *Pioneers*, The Dentan Printing Company, Colorado Springs, Colorado, 1955

Ellis, Edward S. *The Life of Kit Carson, Hunter, Trapper, Guide, Indian Agent, and Colonel U.S.A.*

FitzPatrick, Val. *Red Twilight, The Last Free Days of the Ute Indians*, Yellow Cat Publishing, Yellow Cat Flats, UT, 2000

Foster, Dora. *Colorado Yesterdays*, The Dentan Printing Company, Inc., Colorado Springs, CO, 1961
- - -. *How "Big Tooth Jim" Met Death, Told to the Pioneers*, Colorado Springs Gazette Newspaper, Courtesy Pikes Peak Library District, March 21, 1921
- - -. *Life of First Sheriff, Peak Region Yesterdays*, Colorado Springs Gazette Telegraph, Sunday, May 22, 1960
- - -. *My Childhood Days in Colorado Sunshine*, Dentan-Berkeland Printing Co., Inc., Colorado Springs, CO 1967
- - -. *Then...The Best of the Pikes Peak Yesterdays*, Dentan Printing Company, Inc., Colorado Springs, CO, 1964

Gallagher, Jolie Anderson. *Colorado Forts, Historic Outposts on the Wild Frontier*, The History Press, Charleston, SC, 2013

Getler, Warren and Brewer, Bob. *Rebel Gold, Shadow of the Sentinel*, Simon and Schuster Publishers, New York, New York, 2002

Gray-Kanatiiosh, Barbara A. *Ute, Native Americans* (Series), Checkerboard Social Studies (Children's) Library, ABDO Publishing Company, Edina, MN, 2004

Gwynne, S.C. *Empire of the Summer Moon, Quanah Parker and the Rise and Fall of the Comanches*, Scribner, New York, NY 2014

Hollister, Ovando J. *Colorado Volunteers in New Mexico 1862*, The

Lakeside Press, R.R. Donnelley & Sons Company, Chicago, IL Christmas, 1962

Howbert, Irving. *Memories of a Lifetime in the Pike's Peak Region*, Morris Publishing, Nebraska 1925 (reprinted with permission by the Old Colorado City Historical Society, 2007)

Howbert, Irving. Indians of the Pike's Peak Region, The Rio Grande Press, Inc., Glorieta, New Mexico, 1914

Keehn, David C., *Knights of the Golden Circle, Secret Empire, Southern Secession, Civil War*, Louisiana State University Press, Baton Rouge, LA, 2013

Jefferson, James M., Delaney, Robert W. & Thompson, Gregory C. *The Southern Utes, A Tribal History*, Southern Ute Tribe, Ignacio, Colorado, 1973

Leckie, William H. with Leckie, Shirley A. *The Buffalo Soldiers, A Narrative of the Black Cavalry of the West*, University of Oklahoma Press, Norman, OK, 2003

Lanza, Ruth Willett. Scott Kelly, *Man of Mystery*, True West Magazine, courtesy of the Colorado Springs Pioneers Museum, February 19, 1989

Litvak, Dianna. *El Pueblo History Museum, A Capsule History and Guide*, Colorado Historical Society, Denver, CO, 2006

Mann, Charles C. 1491 *New Revelations of the Americas Before Columbus*, Vintage eBooks, Random House, Inc., New York, 2011

Mathews, Carl F. and Matthews, E.C. *Pioneers Early Days Around the Divide*, Sign Book Company, St. Louis, Mo., 1969

Martinez, Wilfred O. *Anza and Cuerno Verde Decisive Battle*, Second Edition, Mother's House Publishing, Colorado Springs, Co., 2004

McConnell Simmons, Virginia. *Bayou Salado*, Published by the University Press of Colorado, Boulder, Colorado, 2002

McConnell Simmons, Virginia. The Ute Indians of Utah, Colorado, and New Mexico, Published by the University Press of Colorado, Boulder, Colorado, 2000

Merry, Robert W. *A Country of Vast Designs*, James K. Polk, the Mexican War, and the Conquest of the American Continent, Simon & Schuster, New York, NY, 2009

Michener, James A. *Centennial*, Ballantine Books, Random House Publishing, New York, NY, 1974

Michno, Gregory F. Encyclopedia of Indian Wars, 1850-1890, Mountain Press Publishing Company, Missoula, MT, 2003

Millard, Candice. *Destiny of the Republic, A Tale of Madness, Medicine and the Murder of a President*, Doubleday, Random House, New York, NY, 2011

Monaghan, Jay. Editor-In-Chief, *The Book on the American West*, Bonanza Books, Crown Publishers Inc., New York, NY 1943

Murphy, Jan Elizabeth. Outlaw Tales of Colorado, Morris Book Publishing, Guilford, Connecticut, 2012

Olson, Robert C. *Speck - The Life and Times of Spencer Penrose*, Western Reflections Publishing Company, Lake City, Colorado, 2008

O'Reilly, Bill, and Dugard, Martin. *Killing Lincoln*, Henry Holt and Company, New York, New York, 2011

Peters, De Witt C., M.D. Late Assistant Surgeon General, U.S.A., *The Life and Adventures of Kit Carson, the Nestor of the Rocky Mountains, from Facts Narrated by Himself*, W.R.C. Clark & Company, New York, NY, 1953

Pettit, Jan. *Utes The Mountain People*, Johnson Books, Boulder, Co., 2012

Perkins, James E. *Tom Tobin, Frontiersman*, Adobe Village Press, Monte Vista, Colorado, 2005

Pierson, Francis J. *Summit of Destiny, Taming the Pikes Peak Country 1858-1918*, Charlotte Square Press, Denver, Colorado, 2008

Ruhtenberg, Polly King & Smith, Dorothy E. *Henry McAllister: Colorado Pioneer*, Pine Hill Press, Freeman, South Dakota, 1971

Safford, Jeffery J., Professor Emeritus of History, Montana State University. *Three Brothers in Arms, The Philbrooks and the Civil War in the West*, University Press of Colorado, 2004

Sides, Hampton. *Blood and Thunder, An Epic of the American West*, Anchor Books (eBooks), Random House, LLC., Knopf Doubleday Publishing Group, 2006

Simmons, Beth, PhD., *Colorow! A Colorado Photographic Chronicle*, published by the Jefferson County Historical Commission and Friends of Dinosaur Ridge, Morrison, Colorado, 2015

Smith, David P., *Ouray, Chief of the Utes, The Fascinating Story of Colorado's Most Famous and Controversial Indian Chief*, Wayfinder Press, Ridgeway, Colorado, 1990

Sprague, Marshall. *The King of Cripple Creek, The Life and Times of Winfield Scott Stratton, First Millionaire from the Cripple Creek Gold Strike*, Reprinted by Magazine Associates, and Friends of the Pikes Peak Library, Colorado Springs, Colorado, 1994

Sprague, Marshall. *Newport in the Rockies*, Swallow Press, Ohio University Press, Athens, Ohio, Fourth Edition, 1987

St. Clair Robson, Lucia. *Ride the Wind, The Story of Cynthia Ann Parker and the Last Days of the Comanche*, Ballantine Books, Random House, New York, NY, 1982

Stokka, Terry. *A Brief History of Bridle Bit Ranch in Black Forest, Colorado, El Paso County, Colorado*, January 2005

Taylor, John. *Bloody Valverde, A Civil War Battle on the Rio Grande, February 21, 1862*, Historical Society of New Mexico, New Mexico University Press, Albuquerque, NM, 1995

Ubbelohde, Carl & Benson, Maxine & Smith, Duane A. *A Colorado History* (8th Edition), Pruett Publishing Company, Boulder, Colorado, 2001

Utley, Robert M. The Story of the West, A History of the American West and Its People, DK Publishing Inc., New York, New York, 2013

Virga, Vincent, and Grace, Stephen. *Colorado, Mapping the Centennial State Through History, Rare and Unusual Maps from the Library of Congress*, the Morris Book Publishing, LLC., Guilford, CT, 2010

Von Ahlefeldt, Judy. *Thunder, Sun and Snow, A History of Colorado's Black Forest*, Century One Press, Colorado Springs, Colorado, 1979

West, Elliott. *Contested Plains, Indians, Goldseekers, and the Rush to Colorado*, University Press of Kansas, Lawrence, Kansas, 1998

Whiteley, Lee. *The Cherokee Trail, Bent's Old Fort to Fort Bridger*, The 1999 Merrill Mattes Brand Book, Volume XXXIII, Published by the Denver Posse of Westerners, Inc., Johnson Printing, Boulder, Colorado, 1999

Whitford, William Clarke. *In the Civil War, The New Mexico Campaign in 1862*, The State of Historical and Natural History Society, Denver, Colorado 1906; digitized by Google as a part of a project to make the world's book discoverable online

Wismer, David A. with Wright, Gary T. *Shamrock Ranch, Celebrating Life in Colorado's Pikes Peak Country*. Johnson Books, Boulder, Colorado, 2009

Wroth, William. *Ute Indian Arts & Culture, From Prehistory to the New Millennium*, Published by the Taylor Museum of the Colorado Springs Fine Arts Center, Colorado Springs, Colorado, 2000

Index

A

B

Mississippi River 26
Monument Creek 36, 58, 113, 117, 119, 130, 131
Myron Stratton Home 107, 143, 144, 145, 146

O

Ouray 35, 135, 136, 137, 139, 140, 142, 145, 147

P

Palmer, William Jackson 34, 129, 136, 137, 140
Panic of 1857 27
Pikes Peak 7, 11, 24, 25, 27, 29, 31, 41, 49, 53, 62, 73, 78, 95, 96, 100, 103, 104, 117, 127, 129, 131, 132, 140, 141, 143, 144, 148
Pikes Peak Gold Rush 7, 24, 25, 27
Platte River 25, 122
"Prairie Dog" 135
Pueblo County 42, 130

Q

Quantrill, William Clarke 88, 89

R

Red River 57
Reynolds Gang 87
Reynolds, James 71
Reynolds, John 71
Robbins, George 119, 120, 121, 131
Roman Nose 116
Russellville 42, 87

S

Salt Lake City Jim Gang 58, 65
Sam Wah's Laundry 140
Sand Creek Massacre 74, 93, 126
San Juan Mountains 140
Santa Fe Trail 1, 2, 3, 7, 23–26, 28–30, 63, 69, 100
Sharps rifle 66
Sheridan, Philip General 120, 131
Shoup, George 126
Shoup, Oliver 126

About the Author

John Wesley Anderson, MBA, is a published author, storyteller and TEDx speaker. John spent ten years in the aerospace business and retired from Lockheed Martin in 2012 to launch a consulting firm allowing him the freedom to pursue his love of writing, history and the arts. Prior to working in the corporate world, John enjoyed a 30-year law enforcement career including being twice elected to serve as the 26th Sheriff for El Paso County, Colorado (he was term-limited in 2003).

Although John has traveled around the world, including five adventures on a catamaran sailing the Caribbean, three corporate assignments into a combat zone on the Horn of Africa and landed on an aircraft carrier at sea, he remains most fascinated by the rich history and art found in his own back yard in the American Southwest.